HOBBIT
LESSONS

HOBBIT LESSONS

A Map *for* Life's
Unexpected Journeys

DEVIN BROWN

Abingdon Press

Nashville

Hobbit Lessons
A Map for Life's Unexpected Journeys

Copyright © 2013 by Devin Brown

Library of Congress Cataloging-in-Publication Data has been requested.

ISBN 978-1-4267-7602-1

Scripture quotations are taken from The Authorized (King James) Version. Rights in the Authorized Version in the United Kingdom are vested in the Crown. Reproduced by permission of the Crown's patentee, Cambridge University Press.

Illustrations by Gary Morgan

13 14 15 16 17 18 19 20 21 22—10 9 8 7 6 5 4 3 2 1

MANUFACTURED IN THE UNITED STATES OF AMERICA

CONTENTS

CONTENTS

A LETTER TO READERS

Courage is found in unlikely places.
—*The Fellowship of the Ring,* Chapter Three

This is a book for anyone undertaking an adventure and leaving behind a life that has been familiar, comfortable, and predictable. It's for anyone starting a new life where nothing may feel familiar, a life that is sure to be uncomfortable at times and anything but predictable.

Maybe you recently graduated. Maybe you are leaving for a distant country. Maybe you are undertaking a new challenge larger than your tea-at-four world has ever known.

Mr. Bilbo Baggins was an unlikely adventurer if there ever was one. And his story can serve as a map of sorts, pointing out the right direction, warning of potential pitfalls, and opening your eyes to new ways of seeing yourself and the world.

Most of all, the story of Bilbo Baggins is a reminder that you are not alone. The road-less-travelled-by has already been trod by a certain hairy-toed hobbit who has gone before on his own amazing adventure.

In the end, Bilbo discovers *there is far more to him than anyone, including he himself, realizes.* This is the real treasure he finds on his unexpected journey, and this is the treasure he returns home with. His invitation to you is to make a similar journey and discovery about yourself and to acquire a similar, priceless treasure.

A STORY OF LONG AGO

In a hole in the ground there lived a hobbit.
—*The Hobbit,* Chapter One

The adventure and our hobbit lessons begin differently for each of us. My own began with a vacation trip I never wanted to take.

My two brothers were ecstatic. I was the opposite. Our family was going on a two-week camping expedition, a "tour," my parents told us, of the state parks of northern Indiana. And I was going to be stuffed in the back of our Ford station wagon, crammed inside our pop-up camper, and bored to death around a series of cement picnic tables while everyone else was having the time of their lives. I was sure I had been kidnapped from my real family at birth—a family that actually liked staying home, a family that liked sleeping in their own beds instead of on leaky air mattresses.

Though I did not know it, I was about to embark on an unexpected journey that would take me far from the wilds of northern Indiana.

Labeled the *thinker* in our house, I had recently discovered that a good deal of life's unpleasantness—family camping trips, family picnics, and other outdoor family events—could be mitigated *if* you had a strategy. My strategy usually involved bringing a book to read.

A big one.

We were to leave on our camping trip Sunday after church. Beginning on the blue-collar, south side of Chicago where we lived, the first leg of our odyssey would take us a full 90 minutes from home—plenty of time to get there, carefully pick out our little square from the dozens of other identical campsites, set up the trailer, pump up the Coleman stove, eat supper at the cement picnic table, and then basically sit outside until it was time to go to sleep.

The Saturday before our departure was the same as every other Saturday. Piano lessons for each boy (for me, another source of misery) followed by a trip to the public library. Back then you could only check out five books at a time. Five books for two weeks—they would need to be *really* big ones. I don't remember what the fifth book was, but over the years the other four have played a major role in my life.

While the rest of my family was out nature-walking or paddle-boating, I sat at that cement picnic table by myself. Picture me opening a book with a strange title by an author with a strange name—neither of which I had ever heard of. I just grabbed the biggest, thickest books from the Science Fiction and Fantasy section I could find. The four books made up a series, and the first one began with an odd Introduction, one that made it sound like the story had really happened.

This is a story of long ago. At that time the language and letters were quite different from ours of today. English is used to represent the languages . . .

Was this one of those stories based on real events in history? I got out the second book. It also had a similar, real-sounding beginning:

Hobbits are an unobtrusive but very ancient people, more numerous formerly than they are today . . .

And so, not knowing that these kinds of openings are what is called the *narrator's stance*, for about twenty minutes at that cement picnic table in northern Indiana, I thought hobbits were real (albeit little) people who had once walked the Earth, a sort of a lost tribe who, in some out of the way place, still might be around.

As I read on, I gradually realized that J. R. R. Tolkien had *not* based *The Hobbit* and *The Fellowship of the Ring* on real events. I also realized that I had begun a great adventure and that life lessons could be found on almost every page—lessons about persevering, about friendship, and about what was and was not valuable in life.

I worked my way through both these books as well as *The Two Towers* and *The Return of the King* in the two weeks that followed. Without ever leaving our campsite, I travelled to the Shire, Rivendell, Mirkwood, Lonely Mountain, and back again.

While the adventure may begin differently for each of us, once it begins, we are quickly caught up, and like countless others before and since, become part of the amazing tale. During those two weeks, I met and walked with an amazing array of characters— the unforgettable cast of elves, dwarves, wizards, and hobbits that all of Tolkien's readers meet. And I was taught the same lessons every reader learns.

It was not until years later (after I had become an English professor and thought more deeply about such things), that I came to see that while Tolkien's stories were not historically real, they were *true*. True in the sense that what they say about life, real life, is accurate. And true in the sense that the lessons they communicate are not only valid, in our world as well as in Middle-earth, they are also extremely valuable.

J. R. R. Tolkien—who was raised on the parables of the Prodigal Son, the Good Samaritan, and the Lost Sheep—understood the power that stories have to convey truth. He knew firsthand the mysterious way that stories can get beneath our skin, sink in, and affect us in permanent ways. He knew how certain stories will accompany us through life, reminding us why we are here and what is really important.

As Bilbo Baggins journeys from the homey comforts of Bag End out into a larger world, we travel along with him. We see what he sees and feel what he feels. And in the end, we learn what he learns— the lessons we need for our own unexpected journey, the journey of life. Like Bilbo, we learn how to say yes to adventure despite our fears. We learn what it means to join together with friends on a mutual quest. We learn not to be overly fond of certain things even as we learn to see the priceless value of others. And finally, we learn to recognize our own place in the wide world and where it is that we truly belong.

The wisdom of J. R. R. Tolkien, which in this book I am calling *Hobbit Lessons*, comes in a form that is not only deeply moving but also great fun. In the chapters that follow, I invite you to set out on your own unexpected journey as we explore Tolkien's timeless message for the hobbit in each of us. Along with Bilbo—who rushes off with no handkerchief in his pocket, the long contract from Thorin waving in his hand—we, too, can shout:

"I'm going on an adventure!"

Chapter 1

WHEN ADVENTURE COMES KNOCKING,
LET IT IN
(Even If It Makes You Late for Dinner)

I am looking for someone to share in an adventure.
—*The Hobbit, Chapter One*

Adventures come in many forms, but they always mean something new for us. And what is new is always somewhat mysterious. Sometimes we can see adventures coming down the road to us long before they arrive—the adventure of starting high school or going off to college, the adventure of a new job, the adventures of becoming engaged and getting married, the adventure of becoming a parent.

But sometimes adventures appear with no warning, when we least expect them. In the opening pages of *The Hobbit*, adventure seems to be the last thing on Bilbo Baggins's mind.

As Bilbo stepped out his front door after breakfast to take in the glorious day, the sun was shining, the birds were singing, and the grass was growing. Stretching out on the seat by his door, he lit his pipe and sent a perfectly round smoke ring rising lazily up into the blue sky above him.

He had no idea that adventure was about to come knocking.

Adventures in books and movies are loads of fun. As we read about someone else's adventures or watch them unfold on the silver screen, we are ushered into a world of excitement without ever having to leave our comfortable armchair. But who of us *really* wants an adventure in our own life? We may *say* we do. We may even *think* we do. But look at how we typically react when something interrupts our regular routine or requires us to do more than we normally do or be more than we normally are. On a day when we are running late, just the printer running out of ink or forgetting that we needed to get gas can bring us close to a meltdown. A morning when we can't find our homework, our keys, our phone, or our whatever is more than enough drama for us.

So while we might *like* to think of ourselves as the adventurous type, truth be told, like Bilbo, most of us prefer to have our lives be quite predictable, to have everything completely under control, and to know exactly where whatever it is we are looking for is at all times.

Even If It Makes You Late for Dinner

"Adventures?" replies Bilbo to Gandalf, who has shown up on his doorstep looking for someone to join thirteen dwarves on a quest to take back their treasure from the ferocious dragon who currently has it. "Nasty disturbing uncomfortable things! Make you late for dinner!"

And so in the opening chapter of *The Hobbit*, we meet Bilbo Baggins—by anyone's definition, an unlikely candidate for a quest. Someone who does not like being disturbed. Someone who likes to be comfortable or, more accurately, hates to be *uncomfortable*. Someone who likes to have his dinner on time.

Someone who looks more a grocer than a burglar.

Someone who, despite the fact that he has big furry feet and lives in a hobbit-hole in the imaginary world of Middle-earth, is remarkably like us.

Not only does Bilbo like having his meals on time, thank you very much, he, like all hobbits, likes having six of them a day whenever possible. And when we meet him living his comfortable, undisturbed, predictable life at the start of chapter one, it is always possible.

"Sorry! I don't want any adventures, thank you," Bilbo tells Gandalf. "Not today. Good morning! But please come to tea—any time you like! Why not tomorrow? Come tomorrow! Good bye!"

And with that Bilbo closes his perfectly round green door with its shiny yellow brass knob in the exact middle, completely shutting out (or so he believes) the call to adventure he has just been issued.

Gandalf Tea Wednesday.

This is what Bilbo *should* have written down. But being somewhat rattled by his encounter with the wizard on his doorstep and even more so by Gandalf's absurd invitation, Mr. Baggins feels the need for a second breakfast—and which of us wouldn't?—to calm his nerves and help him return to his ordinary routine. But even after Bilbo treats himself to another cake or two, he is still too flustered to remember to record his engagement in the Engagement Tablet he uses for such things.

"Dwalin at your service!"

"Balin at your service!"

The next afternoon, hungry dwarves begin to show up at teatime, like hungry dwarves at teatime. In one sense, simply accommodating Gandalf and the thirteen unexpected dwarves is an adventure in itself for Mr. Baggins, for while he likes visitors, we are told that *he likes to know them before they arrive and prefers to ask them himself.* Nevertheless he rises to the unanticipated occasion and makes room in his little hobbit-hole for the entire company and sets off to find something from his cupboards and cellar to share.

As Bilbo begins to throw together this and that, we are given a hint of the great provender which lines his pantries. Tea and tea-cakes come out, of course, but as more (and more) dwarves appear, the hobbit also produces beer and seed-cakes, coffee and buttered scones, raspberry jam and apple tarts, mince pies and cheese, pork pies and salad, ale and eggs, and to top it all off—cold chicken and pickles.

So what is Tolkien's point here about good food (and the good cheer that goes with it)? One thing Tolkien is *not* saying is that we should all renounce the pleasures of the table and live on nothing but a handful of brown rice and a couple of beans each day.

Quite the contrary.

Tolkien makes it clear that good food shared with good friends is an essential part of a good life. In fact, in Thorin's dying words to Bilbo, Tolkien will have the dwarf tell the hobbit: "If more of us valued food and cheer and song above hoarded gold, it would be a merrier world." By contrast, Tolkien's narrator will tell us that one of the characteristics of goblins, who embody the opposite of all that is right and good, is that they hate everybody and everything.

We could say that the importance of hospitality is one of Tolkien's most important lessons—one that we need to be reminded of today. Beginning with the unexpected party in chapter one with its tea cakes, seed-cakes, and all the rest, Bilbo will share a good meal with all of the good people (and occasionally good animals) of Middle-earth that he meets. With each of the stops he makes, he eats his way across Middle-earth: from the refined hospitality of the elves in Rivendell, to the late night supper (of rabbits, hares, and a small sheep) roasted on the rock shelf of the eagles, to the vegetarian meals (of bread, butter, honey, and clotted cream) in Beorn's hall, to the warm welcome and feasting the company is greeted with at Lake-town.

With its 144 guests and its weeks and weeks of preparation, the long-expected party Bilbo throws at the start of *The Fellowship of the Ring* is even more merry (and its food even more plentiful) than the unexpected one at the beginning of *The Hobbit*. In the opening chapter, we find this description of the hospitality at Bilbo's great birthday celebration:

> When every guest had been welcomed and was finally inside the gate, there were songs, dances, music, games, and of course, food and drink. There were three official meals: lunch, tea, and dinner (or supper). But lunch and tea were marked chiefly by the fact that at those times all the guests were sitting down and eating together. At other times there were merely lots of people eating and drinking—continuously from elevenses until six-thirty, when the fireworks started.

Over and over, Tolkien reminds us that a love and celebration of the good things of creation—and this includes good food—is a crucial part of life. This is seen in the time and care with which he describes the many delicious meals the hobbits enjoy. In fact, the case could be made that Tolkien devotes as much time to the good things the hobbits eat and drink (or wish they could eat and drink) as he does to the battles they fight. We also find Tolkien's celebration of food in the mouth-watering chapter titles he uses, titles such as "Roast Mutton," "A Short Cut to Mushrooms," and "Of Herbs and Stewed Rabbit."

A love and celebration of the good things of creation—and this includes good food—is a crucial part of life.

When adventure comes knocking, let it in—even though it may make you late for dinner.

How can these two principles Tolkien has for us be reconciled?

Tolkien's answer is that there is nothing inherently wrong with a fixed routine or a predictable life. There is nothing wrong with wanting meals to be on time. The problem comes when these desires become so excessive they shut out everything else—as Bilbo does when he shuts his hobbit-hole door on Gandalf. We could say that Bilbo's problem is that he lives in a world that is bounded and limited by the need to be on time for dinner.

If something is going to make him late for dinner, he's not doing it.

In today's world, we might think of someone who starts every day—no exceptions—with getting their coffee. Someone who would be put out, really put out, if something prevented them from getting it exactly the way they wanted, exactly when they wanted it.

We might also think of someone who can't bear to be away from their laptop for more than a few minutes. Or someone for whom being out of cell phone range counts as a real hardship.

Know anyone like that?

When adventure comes knocking, let it in (even if it makes you late for dinner).

Even If Part of You Says Not To

One of the first things we are told about Bilbo is that there is more to him than meets the eye. Plain Mr. Baggins of Bag End is not nearly as plain as he appears. Not by a long shot.

One side of him, which Tolkien refers to as his *Baggins* side, shuts the door on Gandalf and says no to adventure. But he also has, buried (quite) deep down inside of him, a *Took* side, a part of him that has been waiting a long time for the chance to come out.

And this adventure will be just the thing to do it.

We are all very familiar with the Baggins side of Bilbo, because we all have one. This is the voice in us that says:

Don't risk losing what you already have. Play it safe.

Change is highly over-rated (and usually quite messy). Stay in your Comfort Zone.

Adventures are unsettling. Put on your slippers and make some waffles!

If you know that voice, Tolkien has good news for you. Lots of it.

First, there is nothing wrong with Bilbo, or any of us, being cautious. In fact, there are a number of times where Bilbo's Baggins side is critically needed, times where his good hobbit sense saves them all.

Second, more good news. As we will see, in the end Bilbo does not so much *conquer* his Baggins side as he *redeems* it by putting it in proper balance with his Took side—so that both voices have a say. As we will see, when Bilbo returns home in the end, he does not give up the comforts he has loved—his tea kettle and tea cakes, his fancy waistcoats, or his pocket handkerchiefs. In fact, he will enjoy them even more, once they are in their proper place.

Third, Tolkien tells us that deep down in even the most timid hobbit—and by this he means the most timid human as well—there is a seed of courage just ready for the opportunity to sprout. This seed is present in all the Bagginses, Boffins, Tooks, Brandybucks, Grubbs, Chubbs, Burrowses, and Hornblowers—and in all of us. And the adventure that will bring this seed to life is just around the corner.

Finally, Tolkien suggests that the status quo—staying right where we are—might *not* be as wonderful as we perceive it to be. It is clear that the Baggins side of Bilbo's family tree has been in a rut for a long time. ("And what's wrong with being in a rut?" they would ask.) Through his fiction, Tolkien reminds us that *life is far bigger and far more wonderful than we know*—if only we will open the door to it and not put boundaries or limits on what we think we can do.

Tolkien uses a revealing phrase in his discussion of these two sides that Bilbo has. He tells us that Bilbo was *not quite so prosy as he liked to believe*. At the start of the story, Bilbo prides himself on being very business-like (we might say grocer-like). He likes to think of himself as someone who has little or no use for the imagination or flights of fancy because he lives in the real world, the world of facts written down in prose. But, Tolkien reminds us, a life without poetry, a life where choices are *always* practical and business-like, leaves out the best parts.

"I have come that they might have life, and have it more abundantly," Jesus stated. When we meet Bilbo in chapter one, he has life—one that is always safe, comfortable, and predictable. He is living, but he is not living abundantly. We might say that he is living on the wrong side of the comma. One part of Bilbo says to stay on that side. This part says that he should be content with merely living.

Fortunately part of him says the exact opposite.

So what is it that helps bring out the adventurous side of Bilbo, the side that has been asleep or ignored for so long? Tolkien reports that after the bountiful meal is finished, Thorin calls for some music. And then by the flickering firelight, first one and then another—the dwarves begin to sing.

The dwarves' haunting song, which features so prominently in both the book and the film, tells how they must set out before the break of day on a dark and dangerous quest that will take them over the Misty Mountains to dungeons deep and caverns old. As the dwarves sing of the far-off lands of their ancestral home, we are told that something happens to Bilbo. A whole other world is opened up to him. And he is swept away to dark lands under strange skies, to a place very different from his comfortable hobbit-hole. It is then, Tolkien tells us, that the real magic happens.

Something Tookish wakes up inside Bilbo.

Part of the song the dwarves sing tells of the marvelous treasure that once was theirs—pale enchanted gold, gems on sword hilts, objects cunningly wrought long ago. And as they sing, Bilbo feels the love of beautiful things spring into flame and move through him. But this kindling of a love of jeweled crowns and gleaming cups is not the prime effect of the song. Suddenly a desire to see great mountains wells up inside him. He yearns to hear the wind in the pines and to stand beside majestic waterfalls—to carry a sword instead of a walking stick. Most of all he is filled with a hunger to do what he has never done before and explore places he has never seen.

The dwarves' song awakens in Bilbo a longing to become the hobbit he was meant to be. And while in one sense the song seems to cast a spell over him, it would be more accurate to say that it breaks a spell— the spell of fear that has kept Bilbo from doing anything new or anything that might not be considered safe.

If it is a dwarf song that wakes up this other side of Bilbo, the side that wants to do more and be more, what is it that wakes up the adventurous side in you—your own inner Took—and keeps you from always being only practical and businesslike? Maybe it is your favorite playlist coming through the earbuds. Or a fresh breeze on the first day of spring. Maybe you are stirred by a favorite scripture verse or a favorite hymn. Or rustling leaves in the autumn wind. Or simply the encouragement of family or friends saying, "You can do it!" While each of us may have a different answer to this question, Tolkien certainly intends for us feel what Bilbo feels here and simply to be moved by Bilbo's own experience.

When adventure comes knocking, let it in (even if part of you says not to).

Despite What the Neighbors Might Think

If there is one voice in each of us that says to play it safe and a second voice that urges us to do just the opposite and say yes to adventure, there is a third voice that wants to be heard. Certainly Bilbo hears it at the start of the story and hears it very loudly. This is the voice that says, "But what will the neighbors think?"

Tolkien's narrator tells us in chapter one that the Took side of Bilbo's family—because of the way they would go bouncing off on adventures every now and then rather than staying home in their comfy hobbit-holes like everyone else—was not as respectable as the Baggins side. In the Shire, as in our own world, conventionality and conformity are valued by those who see themselves as the judges of what constitutes suitable behavior. Any kind of departure from what is considered normal or proper is frowned upon.

How deep is Bilbo's concern for what the neighbors might think? At the start of the story, it is quite deep, so deep it nearly keeps him from saying yes to Gandalf's invitation to adventure. Tolkien makes a point of telling us that when Thorin addresses him as their fellow conspirator and calls him a most excellent and audacious hobbit, Bilbo is so completely flummoxed, he opens his mouth but no words come out.

Conspirator? Audacious? What would the neighbors say!

"This is a story of how a Baggins had an adventure, and found himself doing and saying things altogether unexpected," Tolkien reports on the opening page. He then adds, "He may have lost the neighbours' respect, but he gained—well, you will see whether he gained anything in the end."

If we skip to the end of *The Hobbit*, we learn that Bilbo has completely lost any claim to being respectable that he may have had at the start. In fact, we are told that he is seen by most of the hobbits in the neighborhood as being utterly strange. At the start of *The Fellowship of the Ring*, Bilbo's reputation has gotten even worse as the general opinion is that he has cracked and gone quite mad. But more importantly, we are told that Bilbo does not mind that he has lost the neighbors' respect. In fact, he no longer is bound in any way by what the neighbors might think about him or even has any interest in it.

And this freedom is part of the treasure he brings home from his journey. This is one part of what he gains in the end.

As Bilbo goes right on with his new life—writing poetry, visiting the elves, and entertaining outlandish folk from distant lands who arrive in the middle of the night and are gone in the morning—he could not care less that he has the scorn (or, at best, the pity) of the highly proper members of his community. Tolkien reports, "He remained very happy to the end of his days, and those were extraordinarily long."

Have you ever really wanted to do something but decided not to because you were afraid of what people might say? Have you ever said no to following a dream because you were concerned that others might not approve? Have you ever felt the pressure to do what is respectable instead of what could be life-changing, instead of pursuing your passion?

When adventure comes knocking, let it in (despite what the neighbors may think).

Very Good for You and Profitable Too

In his doorstep discussion with Gandalf, Bilbo states that the plain folk of the Shire have no use for adventures and concludes: "I can't think what any-body sees in them." After dinner he asks Thorin about such things as out-of-pocket expenses, risks, time required, and remuneration, which is Bilbo's grocer-like way of inquiring, "What am I going to get out of it?"

Just as Gandalf sees something in Bilbo that no one—not even Bilbo himself—sees, the wizard also sees something in the adventure that Bilbo does not see. There *is* a use for the adventure, and it has noth-ing to do with regaining the dwarves' treasure.

Terms: cash on delivery, up to and not exceeding one fourteenth of total profits.

This is the agreement found in the letter that the dwarves leave on the mantelpiece for Bilbo. Af-ter announcing he has decided to send the hobbit on an adventure to Smaug's lair deep inside the Lonely Mountain, Gandalf promises him: "Very good for you—and profitable too."

As it turns out, the adventure is actually *not* that profitable to Bilbo, not in the sense that he returns home with the rightful share of the treasure he was promised. Instead of a one-fourteenth portion of the enormous riches of Smaug's hoard, in the end Bilbo brings home only two small chests, one with silver and one with gold, just what can be easily carried on one strong pony.

So if Bilbo's adventure, in Gandalf's words, is in some way *profitable* for the hobbit, it is only profitable in terms of acquiring a very different kind of treasure, which is exactly Tolkien's point. Tolkien hints at this deeper meaning in the mark Gandalf scratches on the freshly-painted door to Bilbo's hobbit-hole. While typically interpreted to mean burglar, it can also mean *expert treasure-hunter*. It could be argued that Bilbo, like his door, is marked for something special. Bilbo's adventure is, as Gandalf says, very good for the hobbit, but not in a financial way.

The adventure is going to allow a part of Bilbo to come out which needs to come out. Through it he will become the hobbit he was intended to be. We could say that the adventure will be the making of him. The real quest Bilbo goes on was never really a quest for silver and gold—not the literal kind.

So does Bilbo have any sense that the adventure will, as Gandalf says, be good for him?

Tolkien does not answer this question directly, but he does give us a curious hint. At the end of chapter six, Bilbo has an odd dream as he and the dwarves sleep high up on the eagles' rock shelf after being rescued from the goblins. In Bilbo's dream, he is back at his home in the Shire. There he wanders though Bag End from room to room, looking for something which he cannot find.

Through this dream, Tolkien suggests that at this point part-way through the adventure, Bilbo is beginning to have the sense—deep inside of him—that he is missing something. Though he cannot quite put his finger on this something, readers know what it is. What is more, Bilbo also has a growing sense that this thing he is missing is not something that he can find at home. We see a bit farther than Bilbo and know that this missing element is Bilbo's realization of his full potential. We know this could never be found behind him in the life he lived, but will be found only in the adventure that lies ahead of him.

The real quest Bilbo is on is a quest to live more fully. And it is in this sense that the adventure will be very good for him and profitable too.

TAKE A LOOK BACK

HOBBIT LESSON #1: When adventure comes knocking, let it in—even if it makes you late for dinner, even if part of you says not to, despite what the neighbors may say. Saying yes to the adventure will be good for you, and profitable too—though not in the way you might think.

TAKE A STEP FURTHER

1. While few of us will ever go on a quest to take back treasure from a dragon, we have all experienced some of life's great adventures. What are some of the adventures you have faced so far? What adventure is knocking on your door right now?

2. Bilbo is concerned that Gandalf's adventure may cause him to be late for dinner (or, even worse, to entirely miss it). Part of him wants to say no. Part of him is worried what the neighbors might think. What have been some of your concerns when it came to embarking on your own life-changing ventures?

3. Tolkien's point is that what we gain will be worth any hardships we have to endure. What are some of the hardships you have faced and some of the things you have gained through your adventures so far?

Chapter 2

HAVE YOUR FRIENDS' BACKS

(Someone Has Yours)

Fierce as a dragon in a pinch.
—Gandalf's description of Bilbo, *The Hobbit,*
Chapter One

At the climactic end of chapter five, Bilbo finally escapes from the goblin tunnels beneath the Misty Mountains. With the brass buttons of his fancy waistcoat bursting off in all directions, Bilbo gives a terrific *oomph!* and manages to squeeze through the door that leads to the open air and freedom. Still wearing the Ring which makes him invisible (the One Ring cut from Sauron's hand long ago and years later found and then lost by Gollum), he gradually—and silently—works his way down into the valley. As the hoots and hollering of his captors gradually fade away behind him, Bilbo gives a sigh of relief.

He has escaped from the goblins and from Gollum as well!

"I seem to have come out on the other side of the mountains," the hobbit thinks to himself. "Now *where* can Gandalf and the dwarves have gotten to?"

As Bilbo wanders on, an uncomfortable thought begins to come over him. What if his friends are somehow still trapped inside? Minute after minute goes by, and there is no sight of the rest of the company. Bilbo looks at the mountains behind him, he looks down at the magic Ring he now possesses, and he comes to a decision—one made not out of great courage, but out of great loyalty.

He must turn back.

Tolkien's narrator reports that Bilbo, who like most of us has a rather ordinary supply of courage, feels very miserable about his decision. And this is exactly Tolkien's point. *Friends must be willing to do what is difficult, miserable, and even terrifying—if that is what is required.*

To emphasize this lesson, Tolkien repeats it on the very next page. This time as something the dwarves are supposed to learn. Just as Bilbo is about to turn around and retrace his steps back to the very place he least wants to be, he hears voices in the distance. As he creeps forward, he hears Gandalf telling the others that they cannot possibly simply continue on with their journey.

"After all he is my friend. . . . I feel responsible for him. . . . Either you help me to look for him, or I go and leave you here. . . ."

Thinking he will play a trick on the grumbling dwarves, Bilbo sneaks to the edge of their circle, slips off the Ring, and suddenly steps out from the bushes. With the hobbit's appearance, the debate over whether or not to go back for him is immediately ended. But this will not be the last time Tolkien explores what it means to be a friend. Later in *The Hobbit*, Bilbo has to rescue the dwarves after they have been trapped by spiders and then again after they have been locked in the dungeons of the elves. In fact, we could say that the duties of friendship are a lesson that is repeated throughout Tolkien's fiction—and one that must be repeated in our own lives as well.

Over and over, Tolkien will remind us that true friends will always have your back and we must be willing to do the same for them.

At the start of *The Fellowship of the Ring*, Frodo will take great pains (so he thinks) to make sure that no one besides Sam knows of his plans to flee to Rivendell with the Ring. Despite his precautions, his secret is soon uncovered by Merry and Pippin, who announce their intention to go with him on the dangerous quest. When Frodo complains that it seems he cannot trust anyone, Merry—speaking for Tolkien—gives him a brief lecture on the responsibilities that come with friendship:

"It all depends on what you want. You can trust us to stick to you through thick and thin—to the bitter end. And you can trust us to keep any secret of yours. . . . But you cannot trust us to let you face trouble alone. . . . We are your friends."

You cannot trust us to let you face trouble alone. Here Tolkien reminds us that friends are not only required to help whenever help is needed, they are required to help through thick and thin—to the bitter end, even if their help is not asked for.

Soon after the hobbits reach Rivendell, the home of Elrond and his elven kin, the fellowship that will accompany Frodo on the next stage of the quest is selected. Again Merry and Pippin insist on going. *Insist* may be putting it mildly as Pippin declares: "You will have to lock me in prison, or send me home tied in a sack. For otherwise I shall follow the Company."

Elrond claims that two mighty elf lords from his household would be a far wiser choice to go with

Frodo than his two young and inexperienced hobbit friends, but unexpectedly Gandalf disagrees. The wizard argues that in this matter it would be better to trust in friendship than in great wisdom.

And Gandalf is exactly right.

You cannot trust us to let you face trouble alone. Tolkien gives us another illustration of the duties of friendship several chapters later in the climactic scene where Boromir tries to seize the Ring by force, and Frodo decides he must break away from the fellowship and go to Mordor on his own.

As everyone scatters to look for Frodo, Sam is the first to figure out where his master has gone. Rushing down to the boats, he splashes out into the river after him, nearly drowning in the process. Declaring Sam to be "the worst of all the confounded nuisances," Frodo brings the boat around and back to land, with Sam—wet as a water-rat—desperately hanging onto the side.

"That's hard, trying to go without me and all," Sam sputters. "I'm coming too, or neither of us isn't going. I'll knock holes in all the boats first."

Frodo comes to see the rightness of Sam's claim and tells Sam to fetch his pack and join him. As the two paddle off on the last stage of the quest, Frodo exclaims: "So all my plan is spoilt! It is no good trying to escape you. But I'm glad, Sam. I cannot tell you how glad." Then Frodo concludes, "It is plain that we were meant to go together."

And so they were. And this is how *The Fellowship of the Ring* ends.

Though none of us has ever needed to travel to Mordor, we have each had to go on our own minor versions of Frodo's dark and difficult journey. And all of us can certainly think of a time when we were glad to have a close friend, our own version of Sam, alongside us. We can probably also think of a time when someone *insisted* on helping us (whether we wanted their help or not) and in the end we were glad they did.

If Tolkien teaches us that friends have a duty to care for each other *through thick and thin* to *the bitter end*, he also reminds us that these duties are required not just during extraordinary adventures, but also during the course of our normal day-to-day lives. And this is a lesson not to be missed, for in some ways *it is easier to be a friend during a grave crisis or emergency when needs are more obvious and our responsibilities more clear.*

We find an example of this principle at the end of *The Return of the King* after the hobbits come home to the Shire and eventually restore everything back as it was. It is then that—in a reverse of his earlier attempts to abandon Sam—Frodo invites Sam and his bride, Rosie, to come live with him. Frodo explains to Sam that at Bag End there will be "room enough for as big a family as you could wish for." In return, Sam and Rosie care for Frodo as he grows older and the toils of bearing the Ring begin to wear on him. As Tolkien's narrator tells us, "There was not a hobbit in the Shire that was looked after with such care."

Perhaps you have found that in some ways it is easier to be a friend during a crisis when needs are more obvious and responsibilities are more clear than during the course of normal day-to-day life. Tolkien reminds us that the obligations of friendship extend to bad times *and* good.

More on Helping When Help Is Not Welcome

In the last section, we saw that when Frodo tried to leave the fellowship and continue the quest on his own, Sam, out of friendship, had to do *the exact opposite* of what Frodo seemed to want.

In *The Hobbit*, Tolkien has Bilbo face a predicament similar to Sam's.

If Tolkien had wanted to write a simpler story, the climax of *The Hobbit* would have come with the defeat of Smaug as the dragon came crashing down on the Lake-town in flames. Instead, the death of Smaug simply opens the door for his dragon-sickness to spread to men, elves, goblins, and dwarves as each group lays out competing claims for its share of the newly available treasure. And, as Bilbo would say, things quickly become quite impossible.

Of all those who now fall under the spell of greed, Thorin is affected the most. Immediately upon assuming possession of the dragon's hoard, the dwarf king becomes consumed by the desire to hang on tightly to every bit of the treasure—by force if need be. Bilbo watches as the armies encircle the Lonely Mountain, and the desolation of Smaug threatens to become the desolation of Thorin.

It is then that Bilbo decides that he must do something, and this something is as courageous as when he decided he must go back to the goblin stronghold to look for his friends. He decides that for the good of all—*including the good of Thorin and the dwarves*, who have barricaded themselves and the hoard behind a wall—he must give up the Arkenstone, the greatest jewel in the hoard and the heirloom of Thorin's family. Although in this action, we again might say that Bilbo has his friends' backs, Thorin will initially accuse the hobbit of being anything *but* a faithful friend.

At first glance Bilbo's actions certainly *appear* disloyal. He pretends to take Bombur's turn standing watch. Then under the cover of darkness without telling anyone, he scrambles down the wall and makes his way into the headquarters of the opposing forces. When he brings out a mysterious bundle and unwraps it to reveal the Arkenstone, for a moment the hobbit looks very much like a real burglar—not the honest one he claims to be.

"Are you betraying your friends?" Bard asks. As Bard and the Elvenking listen in growing awe, Bilbo explains that his actions were not taken out of any disloyalty to his companions, but out of a desire to bring peace to the warring parties and to break the impasse that is about to bring death and destruction on all sides.

Bilbo is still wearing the armor he was outfitted in after the dwarves reclaimed the hoard. As the Elvenking comes to understand that the hobbit is offering to give up his own one-fourteenth share of the treasure if it might create a way to avoid bloodshed, he declares the hobbit to be more worthy to wear it than many elf princes (though, he admits, the elf princes may have looked more comely in it). Bilbo concludes the meeting by stating that he hopes they will find the Arkenstone useful and then insists on going back and rejoining the dwarves. "I don't think I ought to leave my friends like this, after all we have gone through together," he explains.

As Bilbo makes his way out of the camp, an old man wrapped in a dark cloak rises from a tent door and comes over to greet him. "Well done!" he exclaims, and suddenly the mysterious figure reveals himself as Gandalf, recently arrived from the business that took him to the south. In fact, Bilbo has done extremely well, and Gandalf's words of praise here tell us that Bilbo has fully learned the lesson that friends are of far greater importance than gold and riches. The two exchange a few quick words, and the wizard warns Bilbo of an unpleasant time about to come.

"Keep your heart up!" Gandalf encourages the hobbit before sending him on his way. "You *may* come through all right."

In fact, when Thorin learns what Bilbo has done, things become extremely unpleasant. Declaring him to be a descendant of rats, the dwarf chief lifts Bilbo in his arms and is about to send him crashing down upon the rocks until Gandalf intervenes. Using words not very different from those Frodo said to Merry and Pippin, Thorin bellows, "You all seem in league!"

In fact, Bilbo and Gandalf *are* in league together—in the sense that both of them truly want to help Thorin whether Thorin wants their help or not or even views their actions as helpful.

Gandalf tells Thorin that at this point he is not making a very splendid figure as King under the

Mountain, and readers find it hard to disagree. But as we will later see, Bilbo's example of selflessness will play a major role in restoring his friend's splendor.

Tolkien shows us that it can be extremely hard to help a friend who does not want our help. Most of us can think of a time when this was true for us, as well. Bilbo was called a *descendant of rats* and accused of betraying Thorin. Perhaps there have been times when friends have unfairly called you something derogatory. Maybe, like Bilbo, there was a time when you were falsely accused of not acting like a friend. Tolkien's point is simply that *true friends do what is needed*—regardless of whether their efforts are appreciated or even understood.

That's just how friendship works.

I Am Not Trying to Rob You, But to Help You

One of Tolkien's most moving illustrations of what it means to be a true friend can be found in chapter one of *The Fellowship of the Ring* when Gandalf tries to persuade Bilbo to give up the Ring—the One Ring, which he has secretly possessed for years after finding it deep beneath the Misty Mountains—and leave it behind for Frodo. Like the scene with the dwarves' song mentioned earlier, this scene also figures very prominently in both the book and the film adaptation.

First we are shown how over the years, the Ring has grown to be an increasing burden on Bilbo and has started to affect his relationships with others. We see him using it more and more to avoid contact with people he does not want to see—and except for Frodo, Bilbo wants to see fewer and fewer people. At his farewell party Bilbo confesses to his neighbors and relatives, "I don't know half of you half as well as I should like; and I like less than half of you half as well as you deserve."

He then leaves without a personal good-bye to anyone.

As he finishes his last bit of packing, Bilbo tells Gandalf he is looking forward to moving somewhere where he can finally have some peace and quiet—as if his life in the Shire has been so very disturbed and noisy! Most of all, Bilbo declares, he wants to leave behind a host of relatives prying around and a string of visitors at this doorstep ringing his bell.

No more relatives. No more visitors. At this point in the story we can see that the Ring is having the same isolating and alienating effect on Bilbo that it had on Gollum, the lonely and miserable creature who possessed it for years before Bilbo found it.

The Ring is starting to turn Bilbo into someone *like* Gollum. And Gandalf knows this.

What as Bilbo's friend should he do?

While Gandalf knows that while he theoretically could *force* the hobbit to give up the Ring, this is something he must *not* do. Forcing others to do something against their will is a tactic of the evil folk of Middle-earth. In fact, this is the reason Sauron wants to get the Ring back—so he can have even more power to *rule them all*. As Bilbo's friend, Gandalf can only try his best to encourage Bilbo to give it up.

And this is what he does.

It's not as though Bilbo doesn't know something is wrong. Though he does not look it, the hobbit admits that he is beginning to feel old in an unhealthy way—more stretched than well-preserved, like butter that has been spread over too much bread. More and more he cannot stand to be without the Ring. This, too, reminds us of Gollum. And sometimes Bilbo has even felt as though there was an eye looking at him. But in spite of the fact that he knows something is not right, Bilbo refuses to part with his precious—as he calls it, using Gollum's word for the first time.

"What business is it of yours, anyway, to know what I do with my own things?" Bilbo says to Gandalf with real anger in his voice. When Gandalf suggests that the Ring has too great a hold on him and urges him to let it go—so he can then go himself and be free—Bilbo insists, "I'll do as I choose and go as I please."

What can a friend do in a case like this? How can Gandalf have Bilbo's back without forcing him? Gandalf takes a different tack in his reasoning with the hobbit. He turns to the deep bond of trust and affection they have shared over the years.

"All your long life we have been friends," the wizard reminds him. Then speaking not as a great wizard, but simply as a great friend, Gandalf gently adds, "I am not trying to rob you, but to help you."

A change gradually comes over Bilbo as he looks back over his long life and remembers how Gandalf has always been concerned with his best interests and has always been there for him.

"But I don't seem able to make up my mind," the hobbit protests.

"Then trust mine," Gandalf urges.

And Bilbo does.

Perhaps this scene resonates with you. Maybe you have had a time where, like Gandalf, you tried to persuade a friend to give up something that he or she did not particularly want to give up. Or perhaps you have been like Bilbo here and one of your friends was the one trying to convince you to do something—or to stop doing something. If so, you know that having a friend's back is not always easy. Tolkien's point is that you cannot *force* a friend to do something—even if it's for their own good. You can only try to persuade them to do it and to remind them that you are not trying to hurt them but trying to help them.

Take Such Friends as Are Trusty and Willing

There are passages in a story which take on a special power and poignancy because just for a moment we have the sense that a character is speaking for the author and directly giving voice to the author's own words. Such a moment occurs in *The Fellowship of the Ring* as Frodo talks long into the night with Gildor, the elf lord the hobbits had met by chance, it might seem, as a Black Rider was about to overtake them. Just as Bilbo learned to trust Gandalf, as a wiser voice than himself, Frodo is searching for similar guidance.

Several times Frodo asks Gildor about what he should do, and each time the elf is reluctant to offer a specific answer. Frodo quotes the old saying, *Go not to the Elves for counsel, for they will say both yes and no.* Gildor finally advises Frodo to leave the Shire at once without waiting for Gandalf. And then Gildor adds this recommendation in which we can hear

Tolkien's instruction to us when we find ourselves thrust on a great adventure:

I also advise this: do not go alone. Take such friends as are trusty and willing.

If, as we have seen, one of Tolkien's lessons to us is have your friends' backs, here we find a parallel lesson which is also emphasized in Tolkien's fiction again and again: *Don't refuse the help of your friends—let your friends have your back.*

Tolkien knew that we need this lesson. He knew that for some reason many of us find it is harder to let our friends help us than for us to help them.

Perhaps you are one of those people who struggles with allowing your friends to do something for you—especially when it will require a sacrifice on their part. Perhaps one of your greatest challenges is not being asked to do something difficult for a friend, but having to ask a friend to do something really difficult for you.

Tolkien would tell you that you are not alone.

As we have seen, at the end of chapter three of *The Fellowship of the Ring*, Gildor advises Frodo to let his friends help him on his adventure. One page later at the start of chapter four, we find Frodo pondering the advice he had been so eager to receive just the night before, and deciding to ignore it. He cannot allow his friends to help him on the quest.

That would simply be asking too much.

"It is one thing to take my young friends walking over the Shire with me, until we are hungry and weary, and food and bed are sweet," Frodo thinks to himself. "To take them into exile, where hunger and weariness may have no cure, is quite another—even if they are willing to come. . . . I don't think I ought even to take Sam."

Here again, in case we missed it, Tolkien suggests there is something in us that does not want to accept our friends' help. Those of us who, like Frodo, are uncomfortable letting our friends help us, would do well to start each day by reciting a reverse Prayer of St. Francis:

> Lord, let me allow my friends
>> to be instruments of your peace,
> When I have been hated, let me allow them
>> to bring love;
> When I have been injured, let me allow them
>> to bring pardon;
> When I have doubts, let me allow them
>> to bring faith;
> When I feel despair, let me allow them
>> to bring hope;
> When I am in darkness, let me allow them
>> to bring light;
> And when I am filled with sadness, joy.

In the end it is Sam who convinces his master to listen to the counsel he was given. "You did ought to take the Elves' advice," Sam argues in his homey way. "Gildor said you should take them as was willing, and you can't deny it."

Frodo can't deny it—though from time to time, he will need to be reminded again. After the quest is finally achieved and the Ring is destroyed, Frodo will admit to his faithful companion, "I am glad you are here with me."

And we, too, need to be reminded—some of us reminded again and again—of Tolkien's message: *Take such friends as are trusty and willing.*

Have Your Friends' Backs— Someone Has Yours

If we were all heroes like Gandalf, Bard, Aragorn, or Eowyn—the kind of person who seems to come with built-in courage—once we understood Tolkien's lesson that we are to have our friends' backs, it would be simply a matter of doing it. We would always be there, day in and day out, in normal times and times of crisis, when helping is quick, safe, and easy and also when it is long, dangerous, and difficult.

Unfortunately, few of us are that kind of hero.

Tolkien knew this, and so his lesson has two

parts. The first part is *Have your friends' backs*. Yes, but when the going gets really tough, how can we non-hero types do this? Tolkien's full message to us is:

Have your friends' backs—someone has yours.

Who is this someone? As we look through Tolkien's fiction, a long list of protective figures comes to mind. We think of the obvious characters, characters like Gandalf, Bard, Aragorn, and Eowyn. Beorn also shows up at the nick of time to save the day. We see another kind of unexpected aid in the eagles who come to the rescue several times in *The Hobbit* and *The Lord of the Rings*. Certainly all these characters could be said to have the hobbits' backs at various times.

But Tolkien also wants us to think in larger terms.

The reason that Bilbo is able to help the dwarves—whether they are caught in the spiders' sticky webs, locked in the wood elves' dungeons, or trapped in the tunnel leading down to Smaug's lair—is because all along someone has been helping him. This someone goes unnamed in *The Hobbit* but is definitely present working behind the scenes. This someone is the one Gandalf serves and the one who originally sent the wizard to Bilbo's doorstep on that April morning.

The wizard alludes to this someone in his final words to Bilbo on the very last page of *The Hobbit*. "You don't really suppose, do you, that all your adventures and escapes were managed by mere luck, just for your sole benefit?" Gandalf explains.

And so, along with Bilbo, readers learn that all of the hobbit's remarkable adventures and miraculous escapes were not just lucky coincidences after all. Though at the time it may have seemed like mere chance, they were *managed* by someone—someone who definitely had Bilbo's back and was concerned for all of Middle-earth as well.

In the second chapter of *The Fellowship of the Ring*, readers are given more information about who has been managing events from off-stage as we are told how Bilbo first came to find the Ring, which has now passed on to Frodo. There Gandalf recounts its long background and finally comes to what he calls the strangest event in the Ring's history—"Bilbo's arrival just at that time, and putting his hand on it, blindly, in the dark."

In the words Tolkien gives Gandalf here—*just at that time* and *blindly in the dark*—we again hear the implication that this strange event is far too strange to have happened just by luck. Then Gandalf makes explicit what has been implied. He tells Frodo that the Ring was picked up by the most unlikely person imaginable, Bilbo Baggins from the Shire, not by blind luck or random chance but because there was more than one power at work. Gandalf extends this point, but only a bit, stating that behind Bilbo's finding the Ring there was something "beyond any design of the Ring-maker."

We are not told what or who this something else is, but the use of the phrase *beyond any design of the Ring-maker* suggests the existence of a design crafted by someone else.

Gandalf tells Frodo, "I can put it no plainer than by saying that Bilbo was *meant* to find the Ring, and *not* by its maker. In which case you also were *meant* to have it. And that may be an encouraging thought." Here Tolkien uses italics to make sure we do not miss Gandalf's point. There is something very encouraging about the intentions of this invisible hand because it clearly works for the benefit of Bilbo—it has had his back at each step of the journey.

To underscore Bilbo's coincidental finding of the Ring in chapter five of *The Hobbit*, Tolkien has his narrator jump in to comment: "A magic ring . . . ! He had heard of such things, . . . but it was hard to believe that he really had found one, by accident."

In fact, it *is* hard to believe that Bilbo has found the Ring by accident. It is also very hard to imagine how our Mr. Baggins would have been able to help the dwarves without it. Bilbo needed the invisibility it gave him to lead the spiders off so he could then double back and free his companions. He needed the Ring again to complete his elaborate plan of getting the dwarves into the barrels and down the river. And finally, he needed it once more in order to go alone to face Smaug and discover the dragon's unprotected spot. It is hard to see how the hobbit could have had his friends' backs if all along someone had not had his.

In the episode where Bilbo manages to help the dwarves escape from right under the elves' noses, Tolkien has his narrator point out that "luck of an unusual kind" was with Bilbo. If we look carefully, we see that this unusual kind of luck has been at work from the very start, allowing Elrond to hold Thorin's map up in the special moonlight at the exact time when the hidden letters would appear, making a fish land on Bilbo's feet just when "fish" was the answer to Gollum's riddle, and putting the company outside the hidden door at the only moment the invisible key-hole would appear.

You may wonder how you could ever help anyone else when you seem to need so much help yourself.

You may be the kind of person who thinks *I would like to have my friends' backs, but I have all I can do just to watch my own.* If so, Tolkien has an answer for you. If we learn what Bilbo learns, we, too, come to see that all along someone has always been there, working in ways that are not always apparent, watching out for us. Luck of an unusual kind is with Bilbo and, Tolkien suggests, with each of us as well. And this knowledge—knowing that someone has been and will always be there managing our adventures—frees us to help others.

TAKE A LOOK BACK

HOBBIT LESSON #2: Have your friends' backs—someone has yours.

TAKE A STEP FURTHER

1. Tolkien's message—*have your friends' backs*—is sometimes easier said than done. Think of a time when, like Bilbo, you decided that you must help someone even though it would be difficult.
2. When have you found it difficult to let a friend or family member help *you*?
3. Looking back, Bilbo realizes that someone was helping him all along in ways that are clear only after the fact. Think of a time when you have had a similar realization.

Chapter 3

BE FOND OF WAISTCOATS,
POCKET HANDKERCHIEFS,
AND EVEN ARKENSTONES
(Just Don't Let Them Become Too Precious)

If more of us valued food and cheer and
song above hoarded gold,
it would be a merrier world.
—*The Hobbit,* Chapter Eighteen

The Hobbit opens with Tolkien's wonderful line, "In a hole in the ground there lived a hobbit." The narrator then makes it clear that this is not some dirty, nasty, wet hole with an oozy smell. Nor is it a dry, bare, sandy hole with nothing to sit on. Not even close.

"It was a hobbit-hole," we are told, "and that means comfort."

In fact, to say that Bilbo's hobbit-hole is comfortable is a bit of an understatement.

The floors of Bag End are all nicely tiled or carpeted, its walls are paneled, and if anyone wants to sit, they will find plenty of polished chairs. Its winding hallway leads to a collection of bedrooms, bathrooms, cellars, and pantries—Bilbo has lots of these pantries, we are told. He also has lots of wardrobes. And apparently he needs them, as we are also told that he has whole rooms just devoted to clothes. He is, we learn, particularly fond of fancy waistcoats, what we today would call vests. He also has a strong penchant for pocket handkerchiefs and always likes to have one handy.

Just as the dragon Smaug turns out to have a weak spot in the lining of his underbelly that eventually leads to his downfall, we might say Bilbo's weak spots are fancy waistcoats and pocket handkerchiefs. Or we might say these are *two* of Bilbo's weak spots.

The narrator concludes his opening description by noting—in case we somehow missed it—that Mr. Baggins is quite well-to-do. And the implication is that Mr. Baggins likes being well-to-do and is quite attached to his nice possessions.

We see this excessive attachment after everyone finishes eating in chapter one and the dwarves begin to help clean up. Here readers discover that our Mr. Baggins has another weak spot besides fancy waistcoats and pocket handkerchiefs. Without waiting for trays, the dwarves start to clear the table. To Bilbo's horror, they make "tall piles of all the things" and balance "columns of plates, each with a bottle on the top." Terrified that something will be spilled in his tidy hobbit-hole or that something will get broken, Bilbo scurries around after them squeaking with fright and urging them to be more careful.

Have you ever been so overly worried about something that you own?

The dwarves find the hobbit's excessive concern for his dinnerware and the neatness of his kitchen to be quite comical—so comical (and so excessive) that they make up a song to poke fun at it. "Pour the milk on the pantry floor!" they sing. "Splash the wine on every door! Chip the glasses and crack the plates! That's what Bilbo Baggins hates."

And at this point in the story, this is *exactly* the kind of thing that Bilbo hates. Milk spilled on his beautiful pantry floor, a chip in one of his lovely glasses, a crack in one of his expensive plates—these are his worst nightmares.

And this says a great deal about him.

By the end of chapter five of *The Hobbit*, we find that Bilbo seems to undergo a rebirth of sorts. Earlier, along with the dwarves, he had been taken as a captive of the goblins down into their kingdom deep below the Misty Mountains. Now, wearing the Ring that makes him invisible, he scrambles after Gollum, up the winding passageway that leads outside to the world of daylight and freedom. Finally reaching the door, Bilbo finds that it is partially shut, leaving only a narrow opening he must fit through. Making this even more like a rebirth, we might say.

As Bilbo gives a terrific squirm, everything seems like it is going to squeeze through—everything except the brass buttons on his fancy waistcoat. These, Tolkien seems to be saying, represent a part of the hobbit that must be left behind. Bilbo gives one final push, and with the buttons from his vest scattering everywhere, he steps out blinking into the sunlight.

All right, Professor Tolkien, we get it. The old Bilbo was too fond of his fine-looking waistcoat, especially its flashy brass buttons. He was simply too attached to them, and so they have to go. The new button-less Bilbo who is reborn here has been freed of this excessive attachment.

Except that is not quite how it works.

Four pages later as Bilbo is telling the dwarves the story of how he managed to escape, he gradually gets to the part about squeezing through the door. He looks down *sadly* at his tattered waistcoat and laments, "I lost lots of buttons."

A chapter later as Gandalf is introducing Bilbo to Beorn—as a hobbit of good family and an unimpeachable reputation—we see that he still is having a hard time accepting the loss and is worried about what kind of impression the missing buttons will make.

It seems that our Mr. Baggins has not quite learned the lesson he was meant to learn.

If we jump ahead to the scene in chapter twelve where Bilbo, once again invisible, returns down the tunnel to Smaug's chamber, we find that Tolkien again returns to his message about not being overly attached to material things. Bilbo uses flattery to get the dragon to show off the marvelous way he has armored his soft underbelly. As Smaug displays his finery, Bilbo declares, "What magnificence to possess a waistcoat of fine diamonds!"

On the way down the tunnel, Bilbo had recalled his father's saying that *every worm has his weak spot*. Now Bilbo finds that indeed Smaug has left a bare spot in his vest of precious gems, and it is this weak spot that will allow Bard to defeat the mighty dragon. But we could also say that this weak spot is a manifestation of an even larger weakness Smaug has— the vanity and greed he demonstrates in possessing such a fancy diamond-studded vest.

All right, Professor Tolkien, now we really do get it. It seems that Bilbo did not quite learn his lesson about not being overly fond of fancy waistcoats back at the goblin door. But now *as the hobbit sees his excessive attachment to things mirrored in Smaug's greed*, he finally realizes that he has been suffering from his own, hobbit-sized version of *dragon sickness*, as Tolkien calls it, the spell of possessiveness that afflicts men, elves, dragons, and, for a time, even Bilbo himself.

The Whole Place Still Stinks of Dragon

Tolkien's narrator often assumes a light, grandfatherly voice in *The Hobbit*. Despite this tone, Tolkien intends to convey a serious message through the story about the dangers of greed—showing us how widespread it is, how hard it is to avoid, and how deeply it can afflict any of us.

The defeat of Smaug at the hands of Bard the Bowman leads not to an immediate return of peace and prosperity as was expected, but instead to a gathering of armed forces and a siege of the Lonely Mountain.

A stalemate follows. The armies of men and elves will not retreat without receiving what they consider to be their proper share of the treasure. And Thorin will not give up the smallest piece of the treasure—even if the claim is valid—until the armed camps retreat.

It is here finally that we see Bilbo has truly learned the lesson that Tolkien holds out for all of us to learn as well: that it is all right to be fond of fancy waist-coats, or even of Arkenstones, just as long as we are not overly fond of them, as long as they do not be-come too precious—as Gollum might say.

When Tolkien titles chapter sixteen of *The Hobbit* "A Thief in the Night," its biblical echoes are intended to suggest that in giving up the Arkenstone Bilbo is not a real thief but only *like* a thief in the night. His actions here are secretive and unforeseen, but are not motivated by greed—in fact, quite the reverse. In his most business-like, Baggins-ish manner, Bilbo reminds Thorin that he was told he might choose his own one-fourteenth share of the treasure. And in any case, the Arkenstone has not really been stolen. It will be returned to Thorin as soon as he produces the portion he earlier agreed was rightfully due to Bilbo.

But despite the justness of Bilbo's claim and the crumpled and much-folded contract the hobbit still carries with him, this is not something that Thorin is willing to do. Tolkien's narrator points out "the power that gold has upon which a dragon has long brooded." The spell that the gold under the Lonely Mountain casts is powerful indeed. Smaug has been killed, but his spirit lives on.

"The whole place still stinks of dragon," complains Bilbo, and in his words we hear Tolkien's warning about how greed can be highly infectious.

During the unexpected party at Bag End back in chapter one, Thorin explained how dragons acquire their wealth—by stealing it—and how they jealously guard it as long as they live. Then we are told a detail that is at the heart of Tolkien's lesson about greed as Thorin points out that dragons will sit forever on their hoard and "never enjoy a brass ring of it." Their desire for treasure has nothing to do with any use they will make of it. They desire it simply to be able to say that it is theirs. The only happiness their wealth brings them lies in the fact that *they have it and someone else does not.*

Has there ever been something you wanted simply so someone else wouldn't get it?

We see this principle at work in chapter twelve after Bilbo sneaks down and takes a single cup from the edge of Smaug's great mounds of jewels, gold, and other precious objects. When the dragon wakes and realizes that the cup is missing, the narrator—who has never been at a loss for words—can only state that

Smaug's rage went beyond description and compares it to the kind of rage seen "when rich folk that have more than they can enjoy suddenly lose something that they have long had but have never before used or wanted." Fire streams from the dragon's mouth. He fills the hall with billowing smoke. He shakes the mountain to its roots.

We get the picture.

Tolkien's point is that this kind of extreme possessiveness affects more than dragons. After Smaug is killed, Thorin certainly has far more wealth than he could ever use or want, and yet he still is ready to go to war to keep anyone else from sharing in any of it. Earlier in chapter eight, the narrator pointed out a similar tendency in the elf-king, reporting that "if the elf-king had a weakness it was for treasure, especially for silver and white gems; and though his hoard was rich, he was ever eager for more, since he had not yet as great a treasure as other elf-lords of old."

Though his hoard was rich, he was ever eager for more. Why? Simply because he did not yet have as much as someone else.

Do you know anyone like that?

Just as the men, elves, and dwarves are about to begin fighting each other to determine who will get the dragon's hoard, the goblins and the wild wolves (known as wargs) arrive. This arrival of a mutual enemy who may destroy them all is the only thing that stops the men, elves, and dwarves from destroying one another.

And so begins the battle that no one had expected.

Even though the coming of the goblins and wolves has united the former foes—the men, elves, and dwarves are still outnumbered, and before long the tide begins to turn against them. Bard, the Elvenking, and Dain—who leads the dwarf forces—are each driven back into their own shrinking islands of resistance. All seems lost when suddenly a great shout goes up from the Lonely Mountain. With a loud crash, the wall the dwarves had recently erected to safeguard the treasure comes crashing down and out steps Thorin in full armor at the head of his band of companions.

The evil spell of dragon sickness that infected him has been broken.

If earlier Gandalf pointed out that Thorin was not making a very splendid figure as King under the Mountain—now this impression is reversed. Seeing the armies of elves, men, and dwarves in desperate straits, Thorin abandons the dragon's hoard he has literally been sitting on, and putting aside any thought of his own well-being, he charges into the fray.

As the combat continues, Bilbo is knocked unconscious by a falling rock. When he comes to, the battle is over, and the goblins and wargs have been defeated. The hobbit is quickly brought into a tent where Thorin lies wounded with many wounds. "I wish to part in friendship," the dwarf tells Bilbo and asks forgiveness for the unkind things he had said earlier. Then in Thorin's final words we find Tolkien's message about greed stated once more. He tells Bilbo, "If more of us valued food and cheer and song above hoarded gold, it would be a merrier world."

Here we see that Bilbo is not the only character who has learned not to be overly fond of material possessions. It has taken Thorin longer to come to see what is really valuable in life, but he, too, finally learns the lesson that Tolkien wants us all to learn.

After Thorin is buried and peace is restored among the previously hostile parties, we find further evidence that Bilbo has learned something important about not becoming overly fond of material treasure. When Bard, who is dividing out the one-fourteenth share, tells him, "I would reward you most richly of all," the hobbit makes it clear that he is not interested in any great financial compensation. Bilbo has seen how excessive wealth can produce excessive greed and how this greed can easily lead to bloodshed.

And Tolkien has made sure that we have seen this as well.

Fearing that the violence that Smaug's treasure caused would accompany him all the way to Bag End, Bilbo tells Bard, "How on earth should I have got all that treasure home without war and murder all along the way, I don't know." In the end, Bilbo accepts only a very small portion of the treasure—no more than he can use—telling Bard that it is actually a relief not to have more than this to worry about.

Gandalf accompanies Bilbo on the journey home, and as they get closer to the Shire, they stop to retrieve the gold the company had buried after their encounter with the trolls. Claiming to already have enough to last a lifetime, Bilbo urges the wizard to take it all. But Gandalf, who seems to know something, insists they each take an equal part.

"You may find you have more needs than you expect," the wizard warns the hobbit.

And indeed he does. When Bilbo arrives at Bag End, there is a big estate sale going on. In fact, it is nearly over. Readers learn that after months went by and Bilbo did not return, his relatives had him declared "Presumed Dead." As the day came for the sale, a great crowd gathered—much as a crowd gathered at the Lonely Mountain—all hoping to take home some of the hobbit's lovely furnishings. When Bilbo arrives, we see his closest relatives, the Sackville-Bagginses, already measuring the rooms and planning how they will arrange their own furniture.

Dragon sickness has come to the Shire. Those who had got particularly good bargains are reluctant to even admit that Bilbo is alive. Rather than start a lengthy legal battle, he must buy back many of his own things. Despite this, there are still a good many of Bilbo's silver spoons—hobbit-sized versions of the Arkenstone—that are never accounted for.

In the final pages of the story as Balin and Gandalf arrive at Bag End for a visit, Tolkien gives us a final warning about the dangers of greed. It is seven years since their adventure, and Balin has grown an impressive beard and brings news from the region around the Lonely Mountain.

Where leaders have been unselfish, good things have taken place. The Dale has been rebuilt under Bard, and the valley has become filled once more with people and prosperity. Where leaders have been selfish, the desolation has continued. Balin reports that the old Master of Lake-town has come to a grim end. After having been given a large share of the gold, rather than using it to help those whose homes were damaged, the Master—being the kind that easily catches such disease—fell under the spell of dragon sickness and kept the money for himself. Earlier Thorin was warned that he could not eat the pile of gold he sat upon. Setting out for the wild, the Master is deserted by his companions one by one, and eventually starves to death.

The excessive desire to lay up treasure in Middleearth—whether by Smaug, dwarves, elves, men, Bilbo's relatives, or even Bilbo himself—is one of the most important issues addressed in *The Hobbit*. We could almost say that it is the central issue, for it is the source of nearly all the conflicts in the story.

Professor Tolkien, who was a scholar of Old English, was very familiar with this issue, for it appears again and again in ancient stories like *Beowulf,* where the good king is reminded of his duty to share his wealth with his faithful knights. It is also a central issue running throughout the Gospels, where believers are told to seek first the kingdom of God and that their hearts will be where their treasure is.

Why do we need to be reminded again and again about the dangers of greed? Tolkien never really answers this question. We just do.

My Precious

As we have seen, one of the main messages in *The Hobbit* has to do with the power that gold—or at least our excessive love of it—has to ruin lives and destroy all that is good. Excessive love of gold is at the root of the animosity that exists between the dwarves and elves, as the dwarves still believe that the elves owe them for work done long in the past. It was the great store of gold under the Lonely Mountain that brought Smaug there in the first place. This same gold nearly leads to the outbreak of violence after Smaug is gone.

Of all the gold that appears in Tolkien's fiction, none is more sought after and causes more problems than the golden Ring that Bilbo finds beneath the Misty Mountains. While the Ring is one of the great rings of power—and so is connected to our desire to dominate and rule over others—it is also an object that brings out an almost irresistible desire simply to possess it. Virtually everyone who comes into contact with the Ring struggles with the temptation to take it and keep it for themselves.

In *The Fellowship of the Ring,* readers learn the long history of how Gollum came to have the Ring, a story that began many years before Bilbo's en- counter with him in *The Hobbit.* As the last great alliance of men and elves is able to overthrow Sau- ron, Isildur takes up the shards of his father's sword and cuts the Ring (and the finger wearing it) from Sauron's hand. This is the second time that Sauron has been overthrown, but like a bad penny he somehow keeps coming back. Then, despite the counsel of Elrond, who urges him to cast the one Ring into Mount Doom, Isildur claims it for his own.

We could point out that if Isildur had listened to Elrond's advice and destroyed the Ring then and there, Sauron would have been permanently destroyed and all the bloodshed depicted in *The Lord of the Rings* would have been avoided. Probably we each could point to times in our own lives when if we had listened to someone's advice, we, too, could have avoided many problems.

But, like Isildur, we did not want to listen. Isildur's desire to have the Ring turned out to be greater than his wisdom.

Isildur excuses his seizing the beautiful golden object by saying it is his *weregild*, or payment, for the death of his father and brother. But soon the Ring betrays him, as Tolkien suggests our greed for gold will always do. Surprised by a band of Orcs while out on patrol, Isildur puts on the Ring to become invisible and dives into the river. But while he is swimming, the Ring slips from his finger. As it sinks to the muddy depths, Isildur is revealed to the Orc archers and is slain.

The Ring sits on the river bottom for over two thousand years, until one day two hobbit-like creatures named Deagol and Smeagol decide to go fishing. Deagol hooks a huge fish and is pulled overboard into the water. As he is dragged down near the riverbed, Deagol sees something shining, and grasps it and brings it ashore.

"And behold!" Tolkien writes. "When he washed the mud away, there in his hand lay a beautiful golden ring; and it shone and glittered in the sun." As yet there is no hint of the power the Ring can give to its bearer. Simply because it looks so bright and beautiful, Smeagol immediately desires it. When Deagol will not give the Ring to him, Smeagol takes his friend by the throat and strangles him.

Such, Tolkien would say, is the power of greed.

The Ring betrays Smeagol as well, for when he returns home and discovers, much to his surprise, that it makes him invisible, he takes to thieving, and soon is shunned by all those around him. With no one to talk to, he begins muttering to himself and gurgling in his throat. He is renamed *Gollum* and is cast out from the community to wander on his own, eventually ending up beneath the Misty Mountains.

When we meet Gollum in chapter five of *The Hobbit*, he has had the Ring in his possession for nearly five hundred years, and over the centuries, he has become possessed by it, talking to it like it is a person he loves and calling it his *precious*. We learn that initially he would always wear it, but this tired him. Now, we are told, it is his practice to hide it—not under the mattress of his bed, for he has none—but in a hole in the rock on his little island. This solution also has its problems, for he feels a constant need to go back to check on it to make sure it is still there and still safe.

And Gollum isn't the only one who has this problem of being possessed by his possessions. Have you ever noticed yourself having this same need to always be checking on something that you own? Always wondering *Is it still where I left it? Is it still safe?*

After Gollum loses the Ring and Bilbo comes to possess it, we continue to see its corrupting influence. When Gollum killed Deagol and took the shining band, he justified his claim on the Ring by saying that since it was his birthday, it was due him as a present. Readers learn that Bilbo also makes up his own justification as to why the Ring should be recognized as his. At the end of chapter one of *The Fellowship of the Ring*, when Frodo tells Gandalf that Bilbo told him the story of how he originally obtained it, Gandalf, who understands greed's possessive power, replies, "Which story, I wonder."

It seems that Bilbo felt compelled to fabricate a

story about winning the Ring fair and square in his riddling contest with Gollum. Bilbo's falsehood is an effort to make his claim of ownership stronger than the real truth—which was that he simply found it—and to put his claim to the Ring beyond any doubt.

Gandalf, who all along had sensed something suspicious about Bilbo's account, kept at the hobbit until he finally revealed the truth. Nevertheless, Bilbo still records the lie in his memoirs as the official version. In Frodo's report of Bilbo's odd actions, we hear indications that the Ring was starting to possess and change him. Frodo tells Gandalf, "He told me the true story soon after I came to live here. *He said you had pestered him till he told you, so I had better know too.*"

So Bilbo tells Gandalf the truth *only* when compelled to and then tells Frodo the real story *only* because he fears Frodo will hear it from Gandalf anyway.

Frodo then reports the most revealing and the most un-Bilbo-like aspect of Bilbo's lie. Bilbo insists that the secret of how he really came to own the Ring *is not to go any further* and concludes by telling Frodo, "It's mine anyway."

It's mine anyway—no matter how I came to acquire it, no matter if someone else might have a more rightful claim. *It's mine*—and I will tell whatever lies or stories I need to in order to keep it.

This is how possessions can take hold of us, Tolkien warns, so that we say whatever we need to say and do whatever it takes to never let them go. Frodo tells Gandalf that he does not understand why Bilbo made up a false story and how it was very unlike him.

"I thought it rather odd," Frodo concludes.

"So did I," replies Gandalf, who understands the motivation behind Bilbo's dishonesty. "But odd things may happen to people that have such treasures."

Odd things may happen to people that have such treasures. Look what happened to Thorin when he came to have Smaug's treasure. Look at how Bilbo began to lie and to avoid everyone after he got the ring. The word *odd* here seems to be Gandalf's word for *bad*.

Nearly all of us experience a challenge and some experience a change when we come across some great possession or wealth that we feel we must have. Like Thorin and Bilbo, we, too, may begin to act in an "odd" way—lying or demeaning ourselves and others in order to keep some stash.

From the moment he loses the Ring in *The Hobbit*, Gollum has only one obsession—one that he pursues relentlessly for the next seventy years—namely, to get it back. In the climactic scene in *The Return of the King*, Gollum seizes Frodo, who has been the Ring-bearer on its final stage to the Cracks of Doom, and bites off the hobbit's finger. Holding the bloody finger and the Ring aloft, Gollum dances around in glee, crying, "My Precious! O my Precious!" But with his eyes fixed on the shining gold, his frenzy takes him too close to the crack's edge, and suddenly with a shriek he topples over. Still grasping the Ring, Gollum falls into the fire, his final wail of *Precious* fading away in the depths.

Tolkien's point, of course, is that gold and other expensive possessions have a dark and perilous power to bring out the greed in all of us. And if we let our possessions become too important, if we let them become too precious, they will eventually come to possess us and bring about our downfall.

TAKE A LOOK BACK

HOBBIT LESSON #3: Be fond of waistcoats, pocket handkerchiefs, and even Arkenstones (just don't let them become too precious).

TAKE A STEP FURTHER

1. At the start of the story, Bilbo is shown to be a bit too fond of his fancy plates and his fine waistcoat. While people today might not share Bilbo's excessive attachment for these particular things, what are the things that people in our world today can get too attached to?

2. While the part of *The Hobbit* that tells of dwarves, elves, wizards, hobbits, and a dragon is a fairy tale, its story of greed and the destructive power of gold is one that is all too familiar in our own world. Think of someone you know personally or from the news who suffered a great downfall because of greed.

3. While you might not go as far as Gollum, who is willing to kill to get his precious Ring, do you have something that you find it extremely difficult to be without? What is your version of the *Precious*?

Chapter 4

REMEMBER NOT ALL THAT IS GOLD GLITTERS
(In Fact, Life's Real Treasures
Are Quite Ordinary Looking)

I wish now only to be in my own arm-chair!
—*The Hobbit,* Chapter Eighteen

If Tolkien had wanted to, he could have written a story about someone with an extreme fondness for fancy waistcoats, fine dinnerware, and pocket handkerchiefs, who then goes off on an adventure that changes him into a totally different kind of person who returns home no longer interested in any of these material things of his former life.

But this is not the story Tolkien wanted to tell. In fact, quite the opposite.

When Bilbo sets out in a rush at the start of *The Hobbit*, his biggest concern is that he has forgotten a pocket handkerchief. When he comes back to Bag End at the end of the story, he is shown using a lovely elvish handkerchief to mop his brow—one made of red silk and given to him by Master Elrond himself.

In the final chapter when Balin and Gandalf arrive at Bag End for a visit, the narrator notes that Mr. Baggins's waistcoat is even more fancy than the one he wore on his adventure years earlier. Instead of the brass buttons that were lost on the goblin doorstep, the buttons on this vest are made of real gold. When we see Bilbo some time later as he stands up to make his farewell speech in the first chapter of *The Fellowship of the Ring*, he is wearing a waistcoat which not only is gold-buttoned but also fashioned from embroidered silk.

Clearly the hobbit's fondness for these things has not diminished.

Even his love for his 4 o'clock tea has grown, as we are told in *The Hobbit*'s final pages that the sound of the kettle on Bilbo's hearth is even more musical than it had been in the days prior to his adventure.

So what is Tolkien telling us about being fond of fancy waistcoats, pocket handkerchiefs, and even gold and silver?

If we turn to chapter eight of book II of *The Fellowship of the Ring*, we find a clear statement of Tolkien's position. There Galadriel makes this prediction to Gimli: "Your hands shall flow with gold, and yet over you gold shall have no dominion." A similar observation could be made about Bilbo. He is not called to renounce his luxurious waistcoats, his lovely dishes, his pocket hand-kerchiefs, or any of the other things he has loved. When they are put in their proper place, one which does not dominate him, Bilbo is not called to forgo any of the material pleasures of life, but to enjoy them even more fully and, in doing so, to live even more abundantly.

We see this same pattern in the fact that after Thorin overcomes his excessive desire for the Arken-stone, the precious gem is returned to him—as Bard lays it upon his breast at his burial, where it remains down through the ages.

Tolkien suggests over and over in *The Hobbit* and *The Lord of the Rings* that right living involves *a certain attitude toward the things of this world.* Tolkien's characters are intended to enjoy them, but must be able to give them up if a greater need calls. Our position, Tolkien suggests, should be one of great delight but not slavish adoration. Material things are not inherently wrong. When kept in their proper perspective, they are good. They only become a problem through our excessive attachment to them.

We need to be able to have Galadriel say to us: Your hands shall flow with gold, and yet over you gold shall have no dominion.

But how are we to avoid the greed and excessive attachment that seems to afflict nearly everyone in *The Hobbit*? How do we avoid becoming

Gollumized—with our own version or versions of the *Precious*?

Avoiding greed and excessive attachment is easier said than done. Tolkien gives us a clear illustration of this principle in the opening chapter of *The Fellowship of the Ring* as Bilbo tries to leave the Ring behind on the mantelpiece for Frodo to find. Tolkien devotes three entire pages to recount how difficult it is for Bilbo to do this. In the end, it is only with the help of Gandalf that Bilbo is able to become the first person in the history of the Ring to voluntarily give it up.

A chapter later, as the wizard tells Frodo about Bilbo's excessive attachment to the Ring, Tolkien's point become quite clear. We are reminded of Smaug's excessive attachment to his treasure as well as the possessiveness that Thorin demonstrated once he got it. We may also be reminded of the possessiveness we may have for our own treasure, as Gandalf explains: *Its keeper never abandons it. At most he plays with the idea of handing it on to someone else's care—and that only at an early stage, when it first begins to grip.*

Tolkien's solution for this grip that our possessions come to have on us, his antidote for greed or dragon sickness, can be found in what might be called *the sacramental ordinary.*

As Bilbo nears home at the end of his adventure, he comes up over a rise and sees his own hill off in the distance. He is so moved by this sight, he makes up a poem to praise and celebrate the *ordinary* wonders of the Shire. What has he learned *is really of value* in this world? Not gold and jewels, but the green meadows, hills, and trees that he has known all his life. This is the real treasure.

The priceless value of the ordinary things that surround us is one of Tolkien's favorite topics. If we can see the worth of everyday things, if we can see the sacramental ordinary, then we are not going to be susceptible to the spell of greed.

One of the many times we find Tolkien presenting this lesson occurs as Bilbo and Gandalf finally get to Rivendell on the way home. Tolkien has the elves greet them with a song with this very point.

"The stars are far brighter than gems without measure," they sing. The moon is whiter than silver in treasure. The fire on the hearth is more shining than gold. The green grass is growing in the meadow. The water is flowing in the river. The leaves are blowing in the breeze.

These things that belong to everyone and to no one—these are what Tolkien says should be valued and cherished. And these other things—the gems without measure, silver in treasure, and shining gold—these are *not* what is important.

Another illustration of Tolkien's way of seeing the

extraordinary in the ordinary can be found in the very last line of *The Hobbit*. After an amazing tale of harrowing encounters with trolls, goblins, spiders, and a dragon, Tolkien chooses to leave us with an image of the commonplace, as Bilbo laughs and hands Gandalf the tobacco jar. Sharing laughter and a pipe with a good friend. What could be more ordinary—and more priceless—than this?

What is your own version of Tolkien's sacramental ordinary? Do you have something which might seem common or everyday to others but is worth more to you than a dragon's hoard?

A Tale of Two Treasures

All along, *The Hobbit* has been a tale of two very different kinds of treasure.

One kind of treasure can be stolen—by a dragon, by invading armies, or even (as Bilbo discovers when he returns home) by neighbors and relatives. Because there is always going to be someone else who wants it for themselves, this kind of treasure needs constant guarding. Think of Gollum always needing to go back to his little island and check on the Ring to make sure it is still where he left it. The moment it is out of sight, he begins to worry about it again.

This kind of treasure can also be lost—in Gollum's case, in the pitch black passageways beneath the mountains or, as Isildur found out, while swimming in the river. It also needs constant care, for like Bilbo's fine plates and glasses it can be chipped or cracked, or like his fancy waistcoat it can become torn or damaged.

This kind of treasure *always* becomes a burden in the end, and Tolkien suggests that it can cut us off from others and lead to a life of isolation.

There is one other important fact about this kind of treasure—no matter how much you have, you can never have enough. We get a hint of this in chapter one of *The Hobbit* when Thorin tells Bilbo how the hoard Smaug sits on once belonged to the dwarves.

"We have never forgotten our stolen treasure," Thorin explains. Then as he strokes the expensive gold chain around his neck, he adds, "And even now, *when I will allow we have a good bit laid by* . . . we still mean to get it back."

Have you ever met anyone, no matter how well off, who if you offered them more money, would say, "No thanks, I already have enough" and turn it down? Having a life goal of becoming wealthy is like running in a race where the finish line keeps moving further and further. No matter how far or how fast you run, you never get there. When John D. Rockefeller, one of the richest men in history, was asked how much money it took to make a man happy, his famous reply was "Just a little bit more."

One final contrast can be found between these two types of treasure: if you expect it to make you happy, the gold and silver kind will always betray you. Even if you manage to hold on to it, Tolkien suggests that the real problem with this kind of treasure is that despite its promise to provide happiness, it does not satisfy.

But, Tolkien wants to remind us, there is another kind of treasure—one that will not rust or get chipped or get torn or be eaten by moths, one that thieves cannot break in and steal. Tolkien gives us a glimpse of this treasure in *The Fellowship of the Ring* as Frodo is reunited with Bilbo at Rivendell and the two have their first chat together in a long time. As they slip off to Bilbo's room, the narrator points out that they do not talk of the great events and perils related to the Ring, but instead talk of the stars, trees, and the "gentle fall of the bright year in the woods."

This second kind of treasure, Tolkien suggests, may not look like much on the surface. In fact, it probably will not shine, glitter, or appear to be of much value at all. Tolkien illustrates this truth in chapter nine of *The Fellowship of the Ring*, when Frodo, Sam, Merry, and Pippin finally arrive at the Prancing Pony. At the cozy inn where the hobbits are finally able to have a rest and a hot meal after the first part of their journey, Frodo notices a strange-looking, weather-beaten man sitting alone in the shadows of the common room. His boots are worn and caked with mud. His dark-green cloak is travel stained.

As we and the hobbits come to discover, this strange-looking man is Aragorn, the future king, though at the Prancing Pony he is known as Strider, a name that fits his unassuming appearance. Frodo finally is given the letter that Gandalf left with the inn keeper. In it, the wizard tells Frodo he is to accept Aragorn's help.

"Make sure that it is the real Strider," Gandalf warns. "There are many strange men on the roads."

How is Frodo to know that this is the real Strider? Gandalf writes that there will be a quality of true worth about him—not the flashy kind or superficial kind of worth but something deeper. To help explain what he means, Gandalf quotes a poem that Bilbo, who it turns out is a good friend of Aragorn, wrote to describe this quality he has. The opening line states, "All that is gold does not glitter."

And here we see one more difference in these two kinds of treasure. The first kind of treasure—whether a dragon's hoard or a certain kind of person—will sparkle and glitter and seem quite stunning on the outside, but this surface appearance is a deception. The second kind of treasure may appear to be quite ordinary, but below the surface will prove to be of highest quality.

Not all that glitters is gold. This is the lesson that Tolkien wants us to learn about the first kind of treasure. Appearances can be deceiving. Gold, silver, diamonds, and precious gems are not the treasure they seem to be. The same is true about flashy people.

All that is gold does not glitter. The deception can go both ways. Don't fail to recognize the second kind of treasure just because on the surface it may appear quite ordinary. The treasure of Aragorn's character is this second kind of treasure. As he appears at the Prancing Pony, he is not very impressive to look at on the surface. No fancy clothes, nothing that would mark him as anyone special, just a mud-caked traveler. We might say the same thing about Bilbo, who looks more like a grocer than an adventurer.

We all know people who seem quite striking on the surface—but only on the surface. On the other hand, who are the people you know whose appearance is quite ordinary—nothing flashing or particularly impressive—but who underneath are anything but ordinary?

Perhaps Tolkien's most moving look at this second kind of treasure comes in the very last paragraph of *The Return of the King*—in the author's concluding words to the thousand-page epic—after Sam has said his farewell to Frodo and Bilbo and returns home. As he comes up the hill, the day is ending, and we are told that he sees the yellow light shining from the windows and the fire glowing on the hearth. As he steps inside, Sam sees that the evening meal is ready and he has been expected. Sam's wife, Rosie, draws him near and sets him in his chair at the table and puts their little daughter Elanor upon his lap.

And so the great saga of the Ring ends exactly where Tolkien intended it to—with a homecoming to a warm fire at the end of a long day and a nourishing meal shared with loved ones. These seemingly common or everyday things—which are not flashy and do not glitter—this is the real treasure, Tolkien says.

An Old Story

Perhaps the first thing most people think of when they think of Tolkien is his amazing originality. Even those who are not familiar with Tolkien's work know that he was one of the most creative writers of his time and the father of the modern fantasy genre. Yes, we can find wizards, dwarves, elves, and dragons in the literature that came before Tolkien, but not like the ones we meet in *The Hobbit* and *The Lord of the Rings*. And his hobbits are an entirely new creature, one never seen anywhere previously, characters we immediately embrace and believe in. Perhaps most amazing of all is the place Tolkien created for all these characters to live in, the realm of Middle-earth—an imaginary world that has such depth and authenticity that it comes to feel as real to us as our own world. And if this were not enough, Tolkien also invented entire languages for his elves (and gives us good bits of the languages that his dwarves and Orcs speak) and shows us the special characters the Elves write with.

Despite these evidences of his remarkable creative genius, Tolkien's central message about what is really important in life is *not* something new or one that he invented. It is a message as old as humankind, one he encountered in his reading many times as a boy and was raised to believe.

One story that Tolkien, who loved ancient myths, would have known well is the legend from Greek mythology of King Midas and the Golden Touch.

One day as King Midas was sitting in his counting house, a mysterious stranger appeared and offered to grant the king his greatest wish. Except for his daughter, there was nothing the king loved more than gold. And though he already had piles and piles of it—more than anyone else in the kingdom—he always wanted more. Accordingly, the King asked that he might be given the power so that anything he touched would instantly turn to gold.

"Are you sure?" the stranger asked, as if to caution that this gift might not be as wonderful as it first seemed. When the king assured him that yes, this was his greatest wish, the stranger waved his hand and made it so.

Midas first picked a flower. Immediately it lost its scent and color and became solid gold. Midas was overjoyed. Then he touched a fruit bowl, and the bowl and the grapes inside also turned to gold. When he picked a piece of bread to eat, it too became gold as did the wine in the goblet he tried to drink from.

"What will I do?" thought the King. "I cannot eat or drink."

Suddenly Midas heard the laughter of his daughter as she ran up behind him. Before he could stop her, she clasped her arms around him and immediately was turned into a beautiful, golden, lifeless statue.

Bowed down in grief, the king broke into tears.

He longed to be able to smell the flowers, eat glistening grapes and crusty bread, and drink wine. But most of all he longed to hear the laughter of the daughter he loved.

"Well, Midas," said a voice the king recognized. "Do you have enough gold yet to satisfy you?"

"I hate the sight of it," the king replied. "Why did you ever grant my foolish wish? I beg you, rid me of this terrible affliction."

And the stranger waved his hand, and everything was returned to what it was before. Everything except the king, for he had learned an important lesson about the true value of the ordinary things around us.

Besides this cautionary tale, with its clear parallels to *The Hobbit*, Tolkien would have also known the gospel story of the rich young ruler who could not leave his riches, the story of the pearl of great price, and the story of the rich fool who had such abundant harvests that he could not store it all.

"I know what I will do," the rich fool decided. "I will pull down my barns and build bigger ones, and I will store all my harvest. Then I will sit back and say to myself, 'My friend, you have enough stored away for years to come. Now take it easy! Eat, drink, and be merry!'"

But then God said to him, "You fool. This very

night your soul will be required of you. Then what will happen to all your goods?"

Tolkien would also have known the famous saying that asks, What shall it profit a man, if he shall gain the whole world and lose his own soul?

The lesson about what is really important in life is an ancient one, one that Tolkien had read about and heard about long before he wrote about it himself. But he knew how easy it is for us to forget this lesson and knew our need to be reminded of this truth again and again.

TAKE A LOOK BACK

HOBBIT LESSON #4: Remember not all that is gold glitters (in fact, life's real treasures are quite ordinary looking).

TAKE A STEP FURTHER

1. As we have seen, in Thorin's final words he tells Bilbo, "If more of us valued food and cheer and song above hoarded gold, it would be a merrier world." In the last chapter, you were asked what you were overly fond of—what was too precious to you. What everyday thing would you say that you need to value *more*? Time with friends or family? A simple sunrise?

2. Tolkien's fiction serves as a reminder of the old truths that *not all that glitters is gold* and *not all that is gold glitters*. Why do you think we need to be reminded of these principles again and again? Can you think of a time when you lost sight of what is really important in life?

3. Frodo and Bilbo sneak off to Bilbo's room at Rivendell to talk of the stars, trees, and the gentle fall of the bright year in the woods. These ordinary things have a sacramental quality for them. What other things would you put on the list of the sacramental ordinary?

Chapter 5

RECOGNIZE YOU ARE ONLY A LITTLE FELLOW IN A WIDE WORLD
(But Still an Important Part of a Larger Story)

Roads go ever ever on.
—*The Hobbit,* Chapter Nineteen

For a story intended for young people (though not *only* for young people), *The Hobbit* contains a considerable amount of violence and bloodshed. While some of the conflicts, such as the encounter with the trolls, are cast in a humorous light, Tolkien's story is at times quite scary.

In chapter four, we watch as Bilbo and the dwarves are snatched in the night by a band of creepy goblins and hauled away through a crack in the back of the cave they have taken shelter in. In the daring rescue that follows, Gandalf runs his sword right through the Great Goblin. Bilbo's encounter with Gollum which follows after that is even more frightening because the hobbit must face the slimy and hissing creature all on his own.

Wargs, more goblins, spiders, and a terrible dragon add to the fearsome elements that we meet in the story. Consider this chilling description of Bilbo's encounter with the great spider which Tolkien gives readers in chapter eight:

> He could feel its hairy legs as it struggled to wind its abominable threads round and round him. . . . Bilbo came at it . . . and struck it with his sword right in the eyes. Then it went mad and leaped and danced and flung out its legs in horrible jerks, until he killed it with another stroke; and then he fell down and re-membered nothing more for a long while.

Readers or moviegoers who are used to the modern, highly-sanitized versions of fairy tales, where blood is never shown and any pain depicted is the kind which need not be taken seriously, find scenes like this disturbing.

So what was Tolkien trying to do? Why make *The Hobbit* genuinely terrifying at times?

In a letter to his publisher on this topic, Tolkien acknowledged that an element he called *the terrible* was present in *The Hobbit*. But rather than apologize for it, Tolkien claimed it was necessary to give Middle-earth its authenticity and make it true to the real world. "A safe fairy-land is untrue to all worlds," Tolkien concluded.

The presence of frightening and terrible aspects makes Middle-earth real. A safe fairyland would be false. The same could be said for a sorrowless fairyland.

When Bilbo finally comes to after the Battle of the Five Armies, he is rushed to a tent where Thorin waits only to make amends before dying. "This is a bitter adventure, if it must end so," Bilbo concludes and adds that not even a mountain of gold could make it less bitter. After Thorin breathes his last, Bilbo must turn away and goes off by himself. There he sits alone, wrapped in a blanket, and weeps until his eyes are red and his voice is hoarse.

Why include such scenes of real sadness in a book for younger readers? To paraphrase Tolkien, we might say that a sorrowless fairyland would be untrue to both worlds. If at the last moment Gandalf had raised his staff and with a great poof had restored Thorin to life, it would have seemed false.

Tolkien put terrible and sorrowful elements in *The Hobbit* because these elements exist in the real world. If Bilbo's story is going to be able to help serve as a map for our own unexpected adventures, then it must faithfully represent the dangers and sorrows we will encounter—not sugarcoat them or pretend they do not exist. In addition, we see many days when Bilbo is hungry, cold, wet, and tired. There will also be times, Tolkien suggests, that will not be scary or sad, but will simply be hard.

Don't Get Off the Path (The Wide World Can Be Dangerous and Difficult)

As you are preparing to set out on your own adventure, wouldn't you rather know about the obstacles and difficulties to come? Wouldn't you rather know the truth? Consider these words of caution that Tolkien's narrator offers at the start of chapter four as the company leaves behind the country they knew and reaches the edge of the Misty Mountains—the place where the real adventure will begin:

> There were many paths that led up into those mountains, and many passes over them. But most of the paths were cheats and deceptions and led nowhere or to bad ends; and most of the passes were infested by evil things and dreadful dangers.

Here Tolkien reminds us that many paths in life *are* cheats and deceptions, ones that will lead us nowhere or to bad ends, and we need to make sure that we are not on a path of false promises but one that will bring us to a good place. As Gandalf prepares to leave the company at the edge of Mirkwood, the wise wizard knows how easy it is to go astray. Speaking for the author, he warns Bilbo and the dwarves—and us as well: "Don't leave the path."

In his famous essay "On Fairy-Stories," Tolkien further explained why he included these darker elements in his fiction, elements which other less-honest writers might have left out. There Tolkien maintains, "Children are meant to grow up, and not to become Peter Pans. Not to lose innocence and wonder; but to proceed on the appointed journey."

We are meant to grow up, not remain children all our lives. And if we are to grow up, then we will need to know the truth—good and bad—about life's adventures. We hear this lesson in Gildor's words to Frodo in chapter three of *The Fellowship of the Ring*. "The wide world is all about you," Gildor tells him. "You can fence yourselves in, but you cannot for ever fence it out."

We may try to close our eyes and stop up our ears, and pretend that adventures are not hard and life is not difficult, but in the end, we will not be able to shut out the truth.

The wide world is all about you. You can fence yourselves in, but you cannot for ever fence it out. Has there been a time when you, or someone you knew, tried to put up a fence to hide behind? In the end, how successful was this fence in keeping the wide world out?

Hardships and difficulties—at first it seems to Bilbo like there is no end of them. Early in chapter two of *The Hobbit,* the narrator tells us that it is pouring rain and has been all day. Bilbo's hood is dripping into his eyes, and his cloak is full of water. His pony is tired and stumbles on the rough stones. It is well after tea-time, but there has been no tea.

"I'm sure the rain has got into the dry clothes and into the food-bags," Bilbo thinks to himself. "Bother burgling and everything to do with it! I wish I was at home in my nice hole by the fire, with the kettle just beginning to sing!"

Yes, bother burgling and bother adventures! Of course, over time the hardships and difficulties that Bilbo endures have a positive effect on his character. As he gradually gets used to not being comfortable all the time—to being cold, hungry, tired, and wet— he becomes tougher and complains less. Soon it is

Bilbo who is encouraging the dwarves when their spirits start to sag, and not the other way around.

As he fishes a very soggy Thorin out of his barrel in chapter ten, the change in Bilbo is quite apparent. It is the hobbit who must take charge, telling Thorin: "Well, are you alive or are you dead? . . . Are you still in prison, or are you free? If you want food, and if you want to go on with this silly adventure . . . you had better slap your arms and rub your legs and try and help me get the others out while there is a chance!"

By the time the company reaches the Lonely Mountain, Bilbo has become the acknowledged leader the dwarves turn to whenever a new idea is needed. And this is the way that adventures are intended to work, Tolkien would say. Tough times make us tougher, dangerous situations help us learn how to act courageously, and problems help us learn how to become more resourceful.

Get Out of Your Rut
(The Wide World Can Be Wonderful)

Children are meant to grow up, and not to become Peter Pans. Not to lose innocence and wonder; but to proceed on the appointed journey. Tolkien's statement certainly applies to Bilbo as well. In fact, the whole point of Bilbo's adventure in *The Hobbit* is that he will grow up and replace his narrow point of view with one that is wiser, broader, and more mature.

One of the first things we learn about the Baggins side of Bilbo's family is that they never do anything unexpected. The Bagginses have been stuck in a very narrow rut for a long time. Stuck in their ways of doing things and stuck in their ways of thinking about the world. So stuck that Tolkien's narrator reports, "You could tell what a Baggins would say on any question without the bother of asking him."

This same narrowness is seen in Bilbo in a number of ways.

At the start of the story we are told that Bilbo looks and behaves exactly like a second edition of his solid and comfortable father. He is a chip off the highly predictable, highly respectable, and highly narrow-minded old block. Most of all Bilbo is a resident of the Shire, a place that does not look favorably on those who think or do things differently, a place where any departure from their normal routine is seen with fear and distrust.

Tolkien knew that most of us can identify with Bilbo. Most of us grew up thinking that our way of doing things was the right way, that our high school or town or church or country was the best—and, for example, that our family's steak knives were the proper or normal or real kind, while those of other families were not really steak knives at all.

While it is normal to identify with our family, locality, or tribe, fortunately most of us eventually outgrow this way of thinking about differences. And by the end of the story, Bilbo outgrows his narrowness as well.

"Confusticate and bebother these dwarves!" This is Bilbo's first reaction to the noisy, bearded, hooded, pushy, and otherwise odd band that appears uninvited on his doorstep and invades his hobbit-hole.

"Come along in, and have some tea!" he manages to say. But unlike hobbits, dwarves do not drink tea. They want beer, coffee, ale, porter, and red wine. As Bilbo rushes off to accommodate their requests, we are told *he liked visitors, but he liked to know them before they arrived, and he preferred to ask them himself.*

Strange visitors who arrive unexpectedly and do not drink tea at tea-time! We can see why Bilbo is a bit flustered. The first moment he has to catch his breath, he sits down in the hall, puts his head in his hands, and wonders what has happened and what is going to happen.

Bilbo goes from being a bit flustered to feeling

positively flummoxed as after their meal, the dwarves begin to clean up in anything but an orderly hobbit-like fashion. In their frenzy, Bilbo is convinced they really are going to bend his forks, blunt his knives, crack his plates, and chip his glasses.

But soon Bilbo's attitude toward their strange and different ways begins to alter. First he discovers that he has something in common with his strange guests. Like him, the dwarves also love blowing smoke-rings, and they turn out to be amazingly good it. Then they start playing their strange dwarf music, and much to Bilbo's amazement, he finds it beautiful and enchanting. Something in Bilbo wakes up, and he finds that the wide world with all its differences can be wonderful.

The wide world with all its differences can be wonderful. Remember the first time you ate ethnic food that you really liked? Remember the first time you listened to music that was different from what you normally listened to and found that something woke up in you? How often do you have a conversation with someone who has a different point of view or different tastes than you?

Do you find that you are open to new ideas, or are you stuck in a rut?

If you find yourself stuck in a rut, Tolkien suggests that an adventure might be the perfect remedy.

The narrator explains that this is a story of how a Baggins found himself doing and saying things altogether unexpected. Soon Bilbo finds himself bouncing off on a dwarf pony, sleeping under the stars, visiting distant lands, eating foreign food, and even wearing dwarf mail, *and finding that he enjoys all these things.*

Of all the different characters that Bilbo encounters on his quest, none initially seems more different from him than Gollum, who lives alone in the darkness beneath the mountains, paddling about in his tiny boat eating raw fish every day. And yet, as different as Gollum is, at the moment when Bilbo is about to kill him "a sudden understanding" comes over the hobbit and he is filled with compassion and pity for the miserable creature.

If Gollum and Bilbo had not been barefoot, we could say that the hobbit briefly is able to step into Gollum's shoes and to see for a moment what life looks like from Gollum's perspective. Bilbo's heart is filled with a vision of "endless unmarked days without light or hope" and he sees that Gollum is not *completely* different from him.

Then instead of slaying Gollum, Bilbo is filled with a new strength, and jumps over and spares him.

The importance of this understanding which Bilbo has cannot be over-emphasized. In fact, given Gollum's role in the destruction of the Ring, we could argue that the entire battle for Middle-earth was fought and won in Bilbo's sudden empathy.

In the end, it is clear that Bilbo has lost more than spoons. He has also lost the narrow point of view he had at the start and has come to see that the way he was raised is not the only way to live. His final words to the dwarves are the reverse of his *confusticate and bebother* from the beginning. "If ever you are passing my way," Bilbo tells them, "don't wait to knock! Tea is at four; but you are welcome at any time!"

Invitations are no longer necessary. And tea time is whenever guests show up.

Bilbo has learned to accept and appreciate others who are different from him. His transformation encourages readers to take the same journey to become less narrow-minded and more accepting of the different ways that are found in the wide world.

Seek Help from Wizards and Wise Folk (Also Be Prepared to Go It Alone)

One thing that can be said about almost every adventure—both real ones and those found in books and movies—is that they are nearly always a combination of the heroes doing some things on their own and some things with help from others. This mixture of assistance and self-reliance seems to be a necessary formula for personal growth and for success in the quest.

Bilbo certainly gets help from a number of sources. Beginning with Gandalf, the list of Bilbo's helpers includes Elrond, the eagles, Beorn, the Master of Lake-town, and Bard. Besides offering encouragement and general advice, the wizard must rescue Bilbo and the dwarves from both trolls and goblins. In addition to offering his hospitality on the journey out and on the way back, Elrond is needed to read the moon letters which tell about the mountain's secret door. Twice the company loses everything but the shirts on their backs, and Beorn and the Master of Lake-town must provide the supplies they need to continue. Twice the eagles show up to rescue Bilbo and the dwarves from what seems like certain death.

One of the principles that holds true throughout *The Hobbit* and *The Lord of the Rings* is that *everyone is going to need help at one time or another*. Even the great wizard Gandalf has times when he cannot make it on his own. After he is taken captive by Saruman, we are meant to think that he might never have escaped from the dark tower of Orthanc without help from Gwaihir, the lord of the eagles. Once he is free, Gandalf still requires help, and Theoden gives him the magnificent horse Shadowfax to ride.

After Bilbo has received help from Gandalf a number of times, Tolkien seems to deliberately send the wizard off on some pressing business to the south. This means that the hobbit will have to solve a number of problems completely on his own. His first challenge comes when the dwarves are taken captive by spiders. With nothing but Sting, his magic Ring, and his wits, Bilbo must come up with a way to free them. After Bilbo kills his first spider, Tolkien has his narrator explain: "Somehow the killing of the giant spider, all alone by himself in the dark *without the help of the wizard or the dwarves or of anyone else,* made a great difference to Mr. Baggins."

The second great problem that Bilbo must solve on his own is how to get the dwarves out of the dungeons where the elves have imprisoned them. As Bilbo wanders about invisibly day after day on his own without coming up with any solution, he thinks to himself, "This is the dreariest and dullest part of all this wretched, tiresome, uncomfortable adventure!"

Bilbo wishes that he could get a message for help to Gandalf, but that seems quite impossible. Tolkien's narrator reports, "He soon realized that if anything was to be done, it would have to be done by Mr. Baggins, alone and unaided."

There are many times when Bilbo wishes Gandalf were around. But as any teacher knows, one of the best ways to help pupils is to allow them to face problems on their own. In fact, learning to solve these kinds of trials by themselves is part of what makes them who they are. And Tolkien, who was not only a teacher but also a father, understood this concept and has Bilbo *solve his own problems whenever possible* and receive help *only for things he cannot do on his own.*

Tolkien's message to us is that like Bilbo we are to seek help from others but also be prepared to deal with many of life's problems ourselves. And Tolkien suggests that the help we receive may come from the strangest sources. Consider this passage from chapter five of *The Hobbit*:

> On they went, Gollum flip-flapping ahead, hissing and cursing; Bilbo behind going as softly as a hobbit can. Soon they came to places where, as Bilbo had noticed on the way down, side-passages opened, this way and that. Gollum began at once to count them. "One left, yes. One right, yes. Two right, yes, yes. Two left, yes, yes." And so on and on.

After becoming separated from Gandalf and the dwarves in the goblin tunnels beneath the Misty Mountains, Bilbo has no idea how to get out. The only solution is to follow Gollum—who does know the way and thinks that Bilbo has gone ahead of him.

Strange help indeed.

In *The Lord of the Rings*, Frodo and Sam face a similar challenge and must allow Gollum—again the only one who knows the way—to serve as their guide. Gollum leads them first across the Dead Marshes and then through the secret entrance to Mordor. One thing is sure. Without Gollum's peculiar form of help, Bilbo would never have made it, nor would Frodo and Sam.

Have you had times when you had to solve a problem all on your own? Have there been times in your life when you received help from an unlikely source?

Part of a Larger Story

On the very last page of *The Hobbit*, Balin reports that since the death of Smaug, prosperity has returned to the land around the Lonely Mountain and its people are starting to sing songs about how the rivers will run with gold.

"Then the prophecies of the old songs have turned out to be true!" Bilbo says with amazement and awe because for the first time he realizes that he, little Bilbo Baggins of Bag End, has played a part in a larger story, one which was prophesied in songs sung many years before he was born.

"Surely you don't disbelieve the prophecies, because you had a hand in bringing them about yourself?" Gandalf asks. There is something in us, Tolkien implies, that wants to believe prophecies can only be fulfilled by the actions of someone else. Surely we are not important enough to be part of any prophecy. Not us.

All along there has been a grand plan. And Bilbo, by his choices and his actions, by his refusal to quit and his determination to do what was right, has had a role in the grand plan to end Smaug's long reign and return the land to its former state. Bilbo has been a thread in a great tapestry—admittedly just one thread, but an indispensible one. Without him the picture would not have been complete.

Here on the final page of *The Hobbit*, Tolkien is saying something critical about our own role in the events of the world.

First, each individual is vital. Just as the great events in Middle-earth do not happen apart from dwarves or hobbits, but through them, so too the great events in our world do not happen apart from human beings, but through them—through us. Tolkien suggests that, as hard to believe as it may seem, we each have a role to play in the world's great story.

But at the same time, each individual is just a small part of something larger. "You are a very fine person, Mr. Baggins," Gandalf says, "and I am very fond of you; but you are only quite a little fellow in a wide world after all!"

Have a proper view of yourself, Gandalf seems to be saying. Not one that underestimates your role, but also not one that is overinflated. Don't start bursting those fancy gold buttons on your vest. You definitely had a role to play. But your role was relatively small compared to the great story it was a part of.

Bilbo's adventure has been a means. As we have seen, his own personal growth was one of the ends, but only one. The hobbit's adventure has also been a means for bringing good to the land around Lonely Mountain and to its inhabitants. The two goals were always intertwined.

Bilbo was chosen, not just because the adventure would do him good, but also because he had something good to do for Middle-earth. Through the action of helping to save those around him, Bilbo himself was saved, saved from a life bounded and surrounded by an inordinate need for predictability, safety, and comfort.

It is not only Bilbo who has played a small part, but all of them. Everyone from Gandalf to Thorin to Bard has had a part to play, and in the grand scheme each of their roles is only a small part. But being a small player in a larger story actually enhances each individual's role instead of diminishing it.

You are only quite a little fellow in a wide world after all. Tolkien's readers come to recognize that they, like Bilbo, have a part to play in the good of all the world, one that is a small part of a much larger design. Bilbo responds to Gandalf's statement with a hearty, "Thank goodness!" And so should we.

Thank goodness that our story is not just a loose strand with no connection to the others in the great tapestry. Thank goodness that we are a part of something larger, but not the only part—for that would be a burden.

Yes, thank goodness!

TAKE A LOOK BACK

HOBBIT LESSON #5: Recognize you are only a little fellow in a wide world (but still an important part of a larger story).

TAKE A STEP FURTHER

1. In Gandalf's warning—"Don't leave the path!"— we find Tolkien's suggestions that the world can be a confusing place and it can be easy to go astray. Perhaps you can remember a time when you got off the right path and how you were able to get back on it.

2. Whether we are human or hobbit, there is something in us that wants to insist our way is the right way and any other ways are not just different, they are wrong. We can all think of a time or an issue where our point of view was too narrow. What was it that helped you become more accepting?

3. Going on an adventure always requires some help. Who are the people who have helped you on your adventure?

4. Have you, like Bilbo, ever felt like you were part of larger plan?

Epilogue

FIND THE ENCHANTMENT ALL AROUND YOU
(Even If You Are Not a Wizard)

He remained very happy to the end of his days.
—*The Hobbit*, Chapter Nineteen

There is something about laying our story alongside a fictional one and seeing the similarities and the differences between the two that can either be quite wonderful or quite daunting—depending on which type of story that we choose.

There is a kind of story that can make our own lives seem dull and our role in the world seem insignificant. In it we read about an immensely popular and successful schoolboy or schoolgirl who can do things that can only be described as astounding. They score the winning goal against the team that seemed unbeatable. They ride the horse that everyone thought was unrideable. They catch the uncatchable criminal and defeat the undefeatable foe. Their lives are non-stop excitement, particularly compared to ours. Unlike us, they are friends with famous and important people. Their accomplishments go beyond anything anyone has ever done—especially us.

The problem with this book is that while we find pleasure in reading it, we always return to our own world feeling our life can never measure up. And it can't. We will never catch the uncatchable criminal or ride the unrideable pony. We will never be friends with important people. We turn to this book to leave behind the disappointment and drudgery of real life, but return to a world and to a life in that world which have been made a little less wonderful than before.

Like the gold we read about in *The Hobbit*, these kinds of stories leave us craving for more—for stories with even greater thrills and even more spectacular accomplishments by even more remarkable characters. But no matter how many of these kinds of stories we read, we can never get enough. And our longing for our own story to have meaning and significance is never satisfied.

Fortunately, there is a second type of story which works in a very different way.

This second kind of story wipes away the film, dullness, or dreariness from our world and makes the people and events of our everyday lives more special, not less. After reading this type of story, we do not despise our circumstances, our actions, or our friends for being unspectacular. These stories cast a spell over our world and make everything in it a little more wonderful than before.

We see with a new perspective that our accomplishments are, in a certain sense, quite miraculous and our friends, in their own way, are very important people. Tolkien's great friend C. S. Lewis once wrote that the reader of this second kind of book "does not despise real woods because he has read of enchanted woods: the reading makes all real woods a little enchanted."

The reading makes all real woods a little enchanted. And all real friends a little magical and all real lives a little charmed.

As things in the Shire begin to settle down, Bilbo slowly starts to get back into his normal routine. He loans his dwarf coat of mail to the local museum, where they display it along with their other relics from the past. And he hangs his famous sword, Sting, up above the mantelpiece. He will not be needing these things in the life he leads at Bag End.

Settling back into his favorite arm chair, he sends a smoke ring rising towards the ceiling and gives a long contented sigh as he waits for the kettle to boil. Far from finding his ordinary life a little flat and dreary, he finds there is a dimension to it that was missing before. It has a new depth and richness.

Or perhaps he just never saw it before.

One thing we can say about adventures is that however they turn out, they all have a way of drawing to a close. Once your own adventure comes to an end, will you still be able to find the enchantment all around you even if you are not a wizard? Will you be able to see the extraordinary quality in the ordinary things of life?

Nasty, Disturbing, Uncomfortable Things?

Like Bilbo, you may have thought that you have no use for adventures and may have wondered what anybody sees in them. Bilbo complains to Gandalf at the beginning that adventures can be nasty, disturbing, and uncomfortable. And he is exactly right. But it is precisely *because* they are all of these things that adventures are useful—useful in helping mold us and make us into different people, useful in helping us become who we were meant to be.

A comfortable, undisturbing, delightful adventure would be of no use at all.

In "The Shadow of the Past," chapter two of *The Fellowship of the Ring*, Gandalf explains to Frodo how after his defeat long ago Sauron has gradually taken another shape and has grown to power again. In fact Sauron has become so powerful that he has left his hold in Mirkwood and has returned to once more inhabit his ancient fortress—the Dark Tower of Mordor. Frodo finds all this news so disturbing and distressing he can only say that he just wishes it had not happened in his time.

"So do I," Gandalf responds. And he explains that so do all who live to see such times. But, the wizard points out, that is not for them to decide. "All we have to decide is what to do with the time that is given us."

All we have to decide is what to do with the time that is given us. Tolkien could have had Gandalf tell Frodo, "All *you* have to decide is what to do with the time that is given *you*," but instead he has Gandalf say *we*, and in doing so includes everyone, all of us, in his statement. If we, like Bilbo, have been chosen for a particularly challenging adventure—it is a normal first reaction to wish that these difficult circumstances did not come about during our time, to wish that we had not been chosen.

All we have to decide is what to do with the time that is given us. In Gandalf's words, we find two important truths. The first is that *we* have to make the decision, we ourselves—no one can make it for us.

Just as Gandalf cannot and will not decide for Bilbo, no one can decide for you what you will do with the time and the circumstances that you have been given.

Secondly, we are not victims of bad luck or of blind random chance. We have to decide what to do with the time that has been *given* to us. Your specific place in time and your specific circumstances have been specially assigned to you. Like Bilbo, you have been chosen. And, though it may not be clear until later, you have been chosen for a reason.

In the end, Bilbo comes to have a very different view of adventures than he had at the start. In his final words to Thorin, Bilbo shows that he has finally seen adventures for what they really are—not a dreadful time of testing and torment that we should try to avoid or once into try to get out of the way as quickly as possible so we can get back to our real life, but a true privilege to be involved in, a great gift.

"I am glad that I have shared in your perils," Bilbo tells the dying king. "That has been more than any Baggins deserves." Even here at one of the darkest moments of the quest, after many days of wandering and being lost, hungry, wet, and cold—Bilbo does not wish he had stayed at home. He does not think his unexpected journey was a mistake or a waste of time, but just the opposite.

Will you see your adventure as a privilege and a gift?

What will you decide to do with the time that has been given to you?

Final Words of Wisdom

And so we come to the end of our *Hobbit Lessons*, but certainly not to the end of your adventures or the unexpected journeys you will take in life. The good news is that Tolkien's stories of stout-hearted, comfort-loving hobbits will never be more than an arm's length away, waiting to be taken back down from the shelf and read again and again anytime they are needed. And each time you read them, there will be new lessons to learn and old lessons to remember.

In *The Fellowship of the Ring,* Elrond has two final pieces of guidance for the company as they are about to leave Rivendell on their dangerous and difficult quest. And in Elrond's advice we can hear Tolkien offering some last words of guidance to each of us.

First, Elrond reminds them that though many difficulties lie ahead—and he has not been reluctant to point these out—many wonderful things lie ahead of them as well. "You may find friends upon your way," he tells them, "when you least look for it."

Elrond could foresee that days would come when nothing would go right and it would seem like they were not getting any closer to their goal. On those days, when they least looked for help to show up or something good to happen, help would arrive—in ways they could never have expected.

You may find friends on your way when you least look for it.

As the company crosses the bridge leading out of Rivendell and starts up the long steep path that will take them out of the valley, Elrond calls out after them, "Look not too far ahead!"

Look not too far ahead. At first glance these very last words of advice may seem confusing because in the days and weeks leading up to their departure, Elrond had been urging them to do the exact opposite. Old maps were brought out and carefully consulted. Scouts were sent to gather information from the areas they would be travelling through. And packing lists were checked and checked again to be sure the company would have what they needed for the difficult days that lay ahead.

But when we have done all we can do to prepare, then Tolkien suggests the best thing we can do is to *not look too far ahead*—to look just to what can be done today and where we will sleep tonight. To not worry about what might be around the next bend until tomorrow and to leave the concerns of the future to the future. To trust that each day's strength will be sufficient for the needs of that day. And so we should.

"Look not too far ahead," Tolkien says to you as you close the book on your own Hobbit Lessons. "You're going on an adventure!"

About the Author

Devin Brown is a Lilly Scholar and a Professor of English at Asbury University where he teaches a class on Lewis and Tolkien. He is the author of *The Christian World of The Hobbit* (2012), *Inside The Voyage of the Dawn Treader* (2010), *Inside Prince Caspian* (2008), and *Inside Narnia* (2005). He has spoken at Lewis and Tolkien conferences in the UK and the U.S. and has published numerous essays on Lewis and Tolkien, including those written for CSLewis.com, ChristianityToday.com, SamaritansPurse.org, and BeliefNet.com. Devin earned a PhD at the University of South Carolina and currently lives in Lexington, Kentucky.

What Readers Are Saying About Devin Brown and His Books

Hobbit Lessons
"Devin Brown makes the labyrinthine world of Tolkien's Middle-earth easily accessible. He shows how a love of reading about dwarves, elves, wizards, and hobbits is also good for you."
— **Charlie W. Starr,** author of *Light: C. S. Lewis's First and Final Short Story*

"Devin Brown has established himself as a leading scholar in both Tolkien studies and Lewis studies, combining thorough research and fresh insight with sprightly, readable prose."
— **David C. Downing,** author of *Looking for the King: An Inklings Novel*

"Devin Brown writes with Hobbitish charm and wizardly wisdom. Readers of all ages will delight in his well-turned insights."
— **Philip Tallon,** author of *The Poetics of Evil*

"Devin Brown's uncanny knack for unpacking big ideas is incredibly engaging. He presents important themes in such a way that readers immediately realize they are learning something significant."
— **Greg Bandy,** filmmaker, director of *C. S. Lewis: Why He Matters Today*

The Christian World of The Hobbit
"There has been an abundance of first-rate books examining the Christian dimension of The *Lord of the Rings,* but Tolkien's other bestselling book, *The Hobbit,* has been largely overlooked. That sin of omission has been rectified by Devin Brown, whose book on the Christianity of *The Hobbit* brings this classic book to full, glorious, and graceful life."
— **Joseph Pearce,** author of *Tolkien: Man & Myth*

"The title of Devin Brown's new book is sure to raise some eyebrows. How could a world filled with dwarves, elves, goblins, wizards, and hobbits be considered 'Christian'? Brown uses what we know about the author of the famous children's story, along with his attention to the details and careful wording of *The Hobbit*, to show how J. R. R. Tolkien wove his faith into its pages."
— **Mark Sommer**, Fantasy Editor for HollywoodJesus.com

"In far too many cases, Tolkien's remarkable novels are taken to extremes by readers. Some pronounce no spiritual elements in the stories, while others find Christian symbolism where there is none. Devin Brown's new book *The Christian World of The Hobbit* brilliantly balances those extremes. Tolkien's Christian faith was a vital part of *The Hobbit*, and I'm thrilled such an accurate book finally tells the real story."
— **Phil Cooke**, filmmaker, media consultant, and author of *One Big Thing: Discovering What You Were Born to Do*

"Like Tolkien himself, Devin Brown steals past the watchful dragons of accredited literary culture to explain how Tolkien's works can embody a Christian worldview without preaching or propaganda, and what this has to do with how they lift the heart."
— **Tom Shippey**, Tolkien Scholar, author of *The Road to Middle Earth* and *J.R.R. Tolkien: Author of the Century*

Inside Narnia
"One can hardly imagine a more thoroughgoing, encyclopedic treatment of the first of the Narnia Chronicles."
— **Bruce Edwards**, author of *Not a Tame Lion*

"Devin Brown offers readers a detailed and delightful look at what influenced Lewis's writing of *The Lion, the Witch and the Wardrobe*. *Inside Narnia* should be on the shelf of all serious fans of the Chronicles of Narnia."
— **Don W. King**, author of *C. S. Lewis, Poet*

"Longtime fans of the Chronicles as well as newcomers to the series will find this book both insightful and informative."
— **Jerry Walls**, author of *C. S. Lewis & Francis Schaeffer*

Inside Prince Caspian
"Devin Brown's love for Narnia and his comprehensive knowledge of C. S. Lewis's writings shine out from every page of *Inside Prince Caspian*."
— **Jonathan Rogers**, author of *The World According to Narnia*

"A splendid blend of scholarship and analysis, this book will help every reader understand C. S. Lewis's *Prince Caspian* better than before. Devin Brown provides wisdom and insight in every chapter. He teaches us not only about C. S. Lewis but also about God, goodness, and life."
— **Marvin D. Hinten**, author of *The Keys to the Chronicles*

"Some books are wonderful, but very few are absolutely necessary. Devin Brown's *Inside Prince Caspian* and its predecessor, *Inside Narnia*, are both wonderful and necessary. I recommend them with great enthusiasm and joy."
— **Eric Metaxas**, author of *Bonhoeffer: Pastor, Martyr, Prophet, Spy*

Inside The Voyage of the Dawn Treader
"Like Lewis himself, Devin Brown is someone who adores great stories and effortlessly weaves them through his book. Upon finishing *Inside The Voyage of the Dawn Treader*, readers are hungry not only to read more of Lewis but to read more great literature."
— **Micheal Flaherty**, president of Walden Media

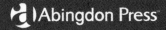